The Time of Life

by

'Lekan Agunbiade

BookBuilders ▪ Editions Africa

© 2019 'Lekan Agunbiade

ISBN: 978 - 978-921-184- 5
E-ISBN 978 978 921 192 -0

No part of this publication may be reproduced,
stored in a retrieval system or transmitted
by any form or by any means, electronic,
mechanical, photocopying, recording, or otherwise
without the expressed written consent of the
the copyright owner.

Published in Nigeria by
BookBuilders • Editions Africa
2 Awosika Avenue, Bodija, Ibadan
email: bookbuildersafrica@yahoo.com
mobile: 0805 662 9266; 0809 920 9106

cover design
Mr. Femi Oloka
Monkmedia, Ile-Ife
+2348112780575

DEDICATION

To GOD
my Source of limitless grace,
my Rescuer and the Lighthouse
to **EVERYONE**
waiting on God for their
TIME OF LIFE
The lord is more than able to fulfil
that which He has declared concerning you.

CONTENTS

Foreword
   Nick Park.. vii

Preface.. ix

Acknowledgments. xi

Abbreviations
Different Versions of the Bible Cited in the Text. . . . xiii

PART I
Hard Times Before the Time of Life

Chapter 1
   The Destiny of the Israelites— Between the
   Pharaoh and the Red Sea 3

Chapter 2
   The Death of Jesus' Friend. 19

Chapter 3
   Abraham's Time of Life.. 41

Chapter 4
   Ruth's Time of Life.. 57

Part II
The Time of Life

Chapter 5
   Is Anything Too Hard for the Lord?. 77

Contents cont'd . . .

Chapter 6
    Beautiful Bethesda of Zarephath. 105

Chapter 7
    The Time of Refreshing. 123

Chapter 8
    The Purpose of Hard Times. 135

Chapter 9
    Farsightedness: A Necessity for
    the Time of Life. 151

Chapter 10
    Nevertheless. 165

FOREWORD

Twenty-five years ago, while pioneering the first ever Pentecostal church in Drogheda, Ireland, I became discouraged by some of my fellow believers and was tempted to give it up. They told me this was an impossible field in which to plant a church—that better men than me had tried and failed. They confidently predicted that I, like my predecessors, would depart a failure with my tail between my legs.

Then God's Word shone into my situation as a sure and certain lamp unto my feet and a light unto my path. I remembered the words of Jesus that we would reap a harvest from where others have laboured and sown (John 4:38). I understood that the laws of seedtime and harvest have been built into the fabric of our earth since the dawn of creation. If others had sown seed, but not stuck around to receive the harvest—that did not invalidate the promises of God. Someone would still reap that abandoned harvest!

And so I determined that I would not only persevere to claim the harvest that would result from my sowing, but I would also claim the harvest of those who sowed and then departed before their harvest arrived. Twenty-five years later, we are still harvesting!

In this timely book, Lekan Agunbiade reiterates that God is working according to a plan, and our Heavenly Leader is eminently trustworthy. Our fallible human

FOREWORD

reasoning often leads us to panic, and if we deviate from the pathway of faith and obedience then we may soon find ourselves falling into the morass of compromise, sin and failure.

Building line upon line, and precept upon precept, the author accumulates a wealth of scriptural examples to remind us of God's unwavering faithfulness towards us, and His abundant record of fulfilling that which He has promised.

Do not allow fear or impatience to rob you of God's manifold blessings! Hold on to His revealed Word! May the book you are now holding in your hands encourage you to persevere by faith and receive your full inheritance.

Nick Park
Senior Pastor, Solid Rock Church, Drogheda
National Bishop, Church of God Ireland
Executive Director, Evangelical Alliance Ireland

PREFACE

As I was rounding up my general nursing training in the autumn 2006, there were 'generous' plans in place to decide my next move – replace a house maid in one location or occupy the vacancy for a house maid in the other location, immediately. Then God showed up! A destiny reforming time in the Castle of Mercy was God's way of snatching me from hopelessness. When the Holy Spirit inspired me in 2008 to write this book, I actually did not know that He was preparing me for future. Some years ago, I remember seeking the face of God regarding who to marry and the Lord would rather tell me the name of my first child but those infallible words of God were all I could hold on to during the tough months we waited for conception and intreated the Lord, the TIME OF LIFE would come for you too. Swapping a jungle ordeal in Eleyele, Ibadan for a wonderful experience in Stockholm, Sweden (within 48hours of darling Sarah Kramer's phone call) remains one of the most urgent transitions I can imagine, but again that is how very fast and instantaneous God can make things to work out – at your Season of life. Waiting is one of the toughest things anyone can go through, especially when no specific waiting time tags have been attached. I still cannot understand why and how that man at Bethesda could wait by the pool side for a whopping 38years – he had been waiting for about

PREFACE

5 years before Jesus was born. We live in the 21st century when joining a 3 people queue at an ATM machine appears like standing for eternity and almost everyone expects the traffic light to be stuck on green so that we keep moving and hastily so. Even in the place of prayer, we expect God to 'speedily teach us patience' and this is more reason we need to remind ourselves of the diverse ways God works. He spontaneously gave children to Penninah but Hannah had to wait for many years; He gave Joseph visions of greatness but had him nosedive and 'forgotten' in the prison; the same Jesus who sent His words to the Centurion's house tarried two more days in the case of Lazarus; the same God who gave Ishmael to Abraham and Moab and Ammon to Lot made Abraham and Sarah to wait until childbearing was physiologically impossible, especially for Sarah.

The book you are holding is not an assembly of motivational stuffs reassuring you that you have nothing to worry about once you are saved – unfortunately, no. However, I am reassured that as you prayerfully journey through the pages of this book, the God that remembered Mordecai will revisit your case and bring you into your **Season of life and boundless joy**.

ACKNOWLEDGMENTS

God Almighty alone deserves all the glory for His wondrous works and grace. Truly, there is no shadow He won't light up – coming after His children. I bless God for making this work possible, at last.

Thanks to Dr. Bamitale Omole for sharing that encouraging revelation from God with me in 2007; the lofty idea became a full manuscript after just 8 days of that monumental discussion of God via Sis Tale.

Mr Femi Olorunmoteni's scolding on 2018 Christmas was the last push that God used to expedite this work, more than a decade after the manuscript had been ready, thank you sir.

I am immensely grateful for the inputs of Prof. Adesegun & Prof. Olawumi Fatusi, our impeccable Agunbiade and Akintilo roots, Mr. Femi Agunbiade, Prof. Jerome Elusiyan, Prof. Morenikeji Komolafe, Mr. Mayowa & Mrs. Feyikemi Popoola, Dr. Akintunde Feyintola, Pastor Sunday Faleye, Dr. Babalola (Babs) Afolabi, Rev. & Rev. (Mrs) Oyinloye, Mr. Dare and Mrs. Tofunmi Ganiyu, Mr. Tolu Adefi, Mr. Olusoga Adebambo and Sarah Kramer.

I am grateful to God for the life changing inputs of Late Chief Adetola Agbe and especially Late Dr Lawrence Omole and his dynasty (Papa Omole saw ahead of these days and gave me two choice items from

ACKNOWLEDGMENTS

his library – a Bible and his autobiography as his contributions to my writing and ministry).

I want to thank our family, friends, colleagues and members of the brethren – especially of Chapel of Grace, OAUTHC, Ile-Ife, Nigeria and everyone who has been involved at one point or the other in the publishing of these works.

I am very thankful to my darling wife – Titilayo for her painstaking efforts and nights of toiling in order to yield near-flawless books. Thanks to the Book Builders Editions Africa, Ibadan, Nigeria for publishing this dream.

ABBREVIATIONS
Different Versions of the Bible Cited in the Text

ASV - American Standard Version
AMP - Amplified Bible
CEV - Contemporary English Version
DBY - Darby Bible
ESV - English Standard Version
GNB - Good News Bible
KJV - King James Version
TLB - The Living Bible
MSG - The Message Bible
NASB - New American Standard Bible
NIV - New International Version
NKJV - New King James Version
NLT - New Living Translation
RSV - Revised Standard Version
WEB - World English Bible
YLT - Young Literal Translation

PART 1

Hard Times Before the Time of Life

From the story of Abraham, we can almost conclude that times of hardship precede the time of life. Having gone through the encyclopaedia to review the histories and courses of great men and women, and having read the Bible to know more about those successful generals in the old and new testaments, one thing I have discovered is that their character was honed from one crisis or the other; they were fine-tuned from having endured troubled waters and hard times.

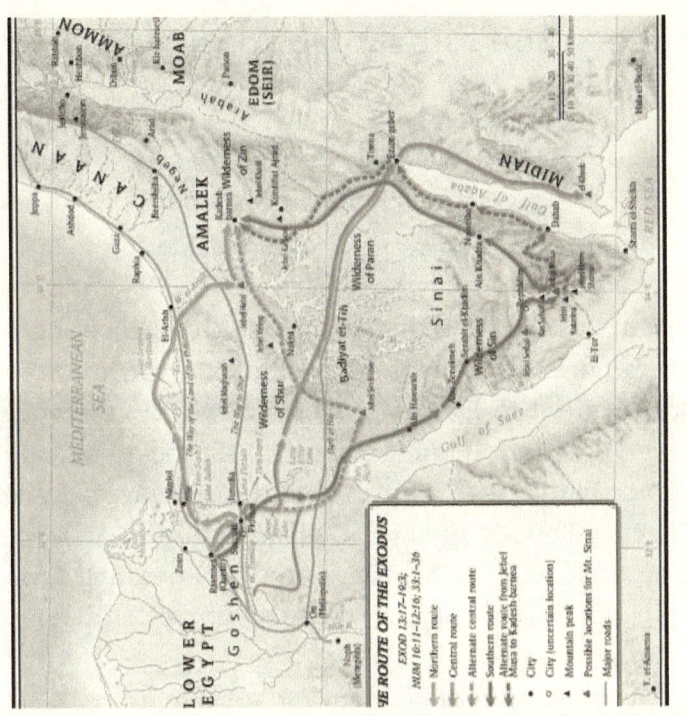
Biblical map of the exodus of the Israelites from Egypt.

Chapter 1
The Destiny of the Israelites Between the Pharaoh and the Red Sea

Now there arose up a new king over Egypt, which knew not Joseph
(Exodus 1 vs. 8)

The events which brought about Joseph's relocation to Egypt and how his father's house and the entire nation of Israel moved to Egypt are well known Bible stories. However, I found it amazing that as the times and seasons changed, the tenure of a king gave way to another in Egypt's history. Despite the exploits and wisdom of Joseph in his days, another pharaoh arose in Egypt who knew not the one time 'Prime Minister' of the land.

> *And Joseph died, and all his brethren, and all that generation. And the children of Israel were fruitful and increased abundantly, and multiplied, and waxed exceeding mighty, and the land was filled with them (Ex 1 vs. 6-7 KJV).*

The Israelites grew in number and might in Egypt as a result of Joseph's character and fortune which paved the way for them to thrive as God was with him and granted him favour with pharaoh. Joseph had been dead for 144 years before Israel left Egypt, and 64 years when Moses was born. The king who began to enslave Israel reigned during the latter part of this 64 years. His policies were in force when Moses was born. His son was possibly the reigning king when Moses came back from the desert to deliver Israel. It is instructive that the Israelites still grew in number even after Joseph's death. This, I am sure, was in line with God's covenant with His people.

> *But the more they afflicted them, the more they multiplied and grew. And they were grieved because of the children of Israel (Ex 1 vs. 12).*

In the face of numerous hardships deliberately devised to restrict their progress, the Israelites rather went ahead to become better than they were and this definitely must have been frustrating to the Egyptian taskmasters and infuriating to the pharaoh.

Before the Set Time of Departure

Every time God decides on a plan, it appears that the first thing He does is look around for people who He can engage to carry out the task at hand. These are men and women who are resolved to die, if need be, in the course of executing God's orders. God sought Moses as his leader and Aaron as Moses' assistant. Moses, however, was not convinced that he was right for the job—not because He did not believe God and not because he did not have a passion for the liberty of his people, but because he feared the Israelites might not believe him, as Moses stammered when speaking. But God, in his perfect and absolute orderliness, had settled all issues concerning this before Moses mentioned them.

> *Now therefore go, and I will be with thy mouth, and teach thee what thou shall say ... And the anger of the Lord was kindled against Moses, and he said, is not Aaron the Levite thy brother? I know that he can speak well. And also, behold, he cometh forth to meet thee ... and I will be with thy mouth, and with his mouth, and will teach you what ye shall do ... and the Lord said unto Moses in Midian, Go, return into Egypt; for all the men are dead which sought thy life (Ex 4 vs. 12-19).*

Indeed, Moses had argued with God, but God revealed His might and how He had planned to raise up Moses for the task ahead. As expected, Moses became confident and courageous in God's plan.

However, one significant thing I learnt is that most of the time, God does not pick on ready-made giants, or some famous men and women, but He usually picks from the seemingly incapable weak and makes giants out of them. He rarely picks from great clans but often from humble ones; He rarely picks the eloquent or 'broad-chested,' but those that are willing; those who can deny themselves of the pleasures of this world so as to please Him. He chooses for Himself 'a colt' or a horse on which no man has ever ridden. Before the episode of the Red Sea, the first task God executed was to recruit Moses and prepare him for task ahead.

Through the Way of the Wilderness

> And it came to pass, when Pharaoh had let the people go, that God led them not through the way of the land of the Philistines, although that was near; for God said, lest peradventure the people repent when they see war, and they return to Egypt. But God led the people about, through the way of the wilderness of the Red Sea; and the children of Israel went up harnessed out of the land of Egypt (Ex 13 vs. 17-18).

The long battle between the pharaoh and the Israelites spans Exodus 5 through 14. I found it amazing that God Himself had hardened the heart of Pharaoh—for a reason that we shall discuss later—but God eventually paved the way for the departure of His people towards Canaan, the land He had promised for them.

Why not take the shorter path?

The Holy Spirit made me understand that the shorter path to their destination was through the land of the

Philistines, but God did not lead His people through that road. God had a purpose for them. God knew them and the limitations of their strength; He knew that peradventure if the Philistines waged war against the Israelites, they might decide to return to Egypt. So God did not lead them through the land of the Philistines. He preferred to lead His people through the wilderness to the Red Sea.

But why would God prefer His people going through a longer route in the wilderness, and worse still to the shores of the Red Sea, when He could have helped them to overcome the challenges the Philistines could pose? Is the Red Sea not a worse option any day? Couldn't the power that parted the Red Sea help in the land of the Philistines and save the Israelites from the stress of the wilderness?

In the midst of these questions, the Holy Spirit helped me to understand that there is no better route to Canaan than through the wilderness. The land of the Philistines, although nearer to their destination, will not only pose challenges in the form of war; it will also divert the hearts of the Israelites to other gods. Their backsliding into idol worship could have much gotten worse had they gone through the land of the Philistines.

I was made to understand that it was out of God's love to keep His people close to His heart and to prove His capability to them at the Red Sea that He preferred to have them travel a longer distance. He therefore led them through the wilderness so that they will not turn back to Egypt upon reaching Philistia.

However unpleasant the wilderness experience is to your course, always remember that God, in His incomprehensible wisdom, has the best in mind for you, even though you may have to pas through a wilderness. If you decide to go through a shorter route, you may easily find yourself in the pit.

Our generation is presently witnessing an age in which people want rapid responses to all issues. Even the so-called Christians want "wait and get" answers which invariably make us force God to work with our 'threats' and 'quit notices' in case He delays His answers. Expressions such as "if you are God . . .", "if your words are true . . .", "prove yourself as God . . .", "if you are still alive . . ." and many more, have become household phrases in our churches and homes, especially when there is an urgent issue we must deal with.

I must say here, as a matter of necessity, that whether God decides to answer your prayers or not, does not enthrone or dethrone Him. He does what pleases Him and He blesses what He does. Realise that God has the best in mind for you; your understanding of the purpose of your journey through the wilderness will strengthen your resolve and build your character. When the strength of others fall, yours will soar. The more the afflictions and stress, the stronger you will be. Understand this and do not run away: *bypassing the wilderness can amount to bypassing your time of life.*

. . . of the Red Sea

> *And the LORD went before them by day in a pillar of a cloud, to lead them the way, and by night in a pillar of fire, to give them light; to go by day and night. He took not away the pillar of the cloud by day, or the pillar of fire by night, from before the people (Ex 13 vs. 21-22 KJV).*

It must be known that the greatest privilege an individual can have is to be led by God both day and night and to have God as one's companion at all times. Even if the situation seems turbulent, having God by your side, means it is, nevertheless, a time of life.

> *And the LORD spake unto Moses, saying, speak unto the children of Israel, that they turn and encamp before Pihahiroth, between Migdol and the Sea, over against Baalzephon: before it shall ye encamp by the Sea. (Ex 14 vs. 1-2 KJV)*

Having led them through Succoth, and Etham, God told His people to encamp at Pihahiroth which was a place by the Red Sea near Migdol—Migdol is a fortress that served to defend Egypt from Asia. The events that took place in pharaoh's palace (Ex 14 vs. 3-9) were, of course, not known to the Israelites; but it was part of God's plan, for He was the power behind pharaoh's stubbornness.

I spent some time thinking about Pihahiroth. Why didn't Moses ask God questions, at this stage, on why they should camp by the seaside? Despite knowing that Pihahiroth was not their destination and that there was no way forward, only the Red Sea and there was no way back. Moses, now the trusting servant of God, did not question God's wisdom and directives. It was Moses' personal decision not to disobey or argue with God despite being trapped between pharaoh's army and the sea.

> *The enemy said, I will pursue, I will overtake, I will divide the spoil, my lust shall be satisfied upon them; I will draw my sword, my hand shall destroy them (Ex 15 vs. 9 KJV).*
>
> *And he made ready his chariot, and took his people with him; and he took six hundred chosen chariots and all the chariots of Egypt and captains over every one of them (Ex 14 vs. 6-7 KJV).*

Pharaoh had six things in mind in this chase:
- Pursue
- Overtake
- Divide the spoils
- Be satisfied with the spoils
- Draw out his sword
- Destroy the people of God

And to achieve these targets, he charged his army to pursue the Israelites. The Egyptian army had four levels:

- Pharaoh, the commander-in-chief
- The chief officers of his immediate household
- 600 chosen chariots—comprising the king's guard and the pride of Egypt
- All the other chariots of Egypt as the main body of the army, including chariot drivers and combatants in each chariot.

Josephus says that pharaoh had 50,000 horsemen and 200,000 footmen. According to Exodus 14, vs. 7, all these must have been divisions of the army. All of these units would have heeded the pharaoh's commands in pursuing God's people.

> *And when Pharaoh drew nigh, the children of Israel lifted up their eyes, and behold, the Egyptians marched after them; and they were sore afraid; and the children of Israel cried unto the LORD. And they said unto Moses, because there were no graves in Egypt, hast thou taken us away to die in the wilderness? Wherefore hast thou dealt thus with us, to carry us forth out of Egypt? Is not this the word that we did tell thee in Egypt, saying, let us alone, that we*

may serve the Egyptians, than we should die in the wilderness. (Ex 14 vs 10-12)

Realising that pharaoh and his men were after them, the children of Israel reacted in three ways:

First, *They were sore afraid.* This is neither unexpected nor surprising. I asked myself, "How did Moses feel when he saw the Egyptian army?" Although the Bible did not record Moses as being afraid, does not, to me, seem enough to conclude that those who did were cowards. They were simply being human. Knowing how wicked, cruel and horrible pharaoh could be and seeing how he had brutalized them, they must have seen that day as their last and would have thought that if they would at all live after that day, it would definitely be as beasts of burden to the pharaoh. The sight of the Egyptian host made them forget everything God had done for them, particularly how God had afflicted the Egyptians for their sake. They forgot how God had been their companion in the course of their journey. Their looming disaster got their undivided attention, not the unseen Deliverer.

Second, *the people cried out unto the LORD.* The content of their cry was not stated in the passage. But "cried out" should make us imagine that they did not just shout; they must have shouted at the top of their lungs. 'Cried out unto the LORD' in most Bible passages means "prayed" or "made earnest supplications". However, considering the fear they expressed and their outrage against Moses, it is a fair possibility that they could have challenged God in the manner they challenged His servant. But if they had actually prayed to Him for help, they would have acted more nobly than they did.

Third, *They complained against Moses.* Considering their choice of words above, one may feel sorry for Moses as the leader of this furious crowd. A better part of the children of Israel must have raised their voices challenging Moses with tough questions which revealed their regret for following Moses out of Egypt. It was painful to read God's own people, God's dear people, preferring to die as slaves in Egypt than to die as free men in God's will. John Dickinson reframed Thomas Jefferson's words in 1775 as, "we resolved and persevered to die as free men than to live as slaves,". But the reverse was the case for the Israelites.

It must be said at this juncture that the children of Israel were only being human in their reaction to the Egyptian army. The foot soldiers, horsemen and 600 chariots led by the pharaoh would shake any human's faith in a miracle to their roots. Little wonder they were already talking about graves in Egypt and a mass burial under pharaoh's torture in the wilderness.

> *And Moses said unto the people, fear ye not, stand still, and see the salvation of the LORD, which he will shew to you today: for the Egyptians whom ye have seen today, ye shall see them again no more forever. The LORD shall fight for you and ye shall hold your peace (Ex 14 vs. 13-14 KJV).*

It is not stated anywhere in the Bible that God had spoken to reassure Moses of what lie ahead at the shore of the Red Sea. Moses must have seen the pharaoh's looming army just as the children of Israel saw them, but how Moses was able to compose himself and address the Israelites after the harsh criticisms they hurled at him, caught my breath. No, those words required more than an eloquent tongue! They required more than skills and courage a leader is expected to possess. They must have come out of Moses' confidence in his unfailing trust in God.

He knew quite well that God would not have led them to the Red Sea only for the pharaoh to come and slaughter them. He knew that either of two things would happen: the children of Israel being empowered by God to overcome the Egyptians—by fighting directly or plaguing the Egyptians again—or by paving a mysterious 'way-out' for His people. In short, Moses was confident that the pharaoh would not have his aims fulfilled. As I keep wondering at Moses' brave response, the Holy Spirit opened Ex 15 vs. 7 to me: *And in the greatness of thine Excellency thou had overthrown them that rose up against thee . . . .*

He did not picture the pharaoh and his chariots as challenging to the children of Israel. Rather, he saw them charging God into battle. Thus, knowing the capacity and winning records of God, Moses was so sure that God, who had never failed, would not start failing at the shores of the Red Sea. The direct implication of this is that even though your present situation may not look like you are on the winning path, your knowledge of God and His antecedents will be crucial to your rescue and will strengthen your resolve that God cannot fail, whatever happens.

You might even become convinced, in bitter situations and tough circumstances, that God can start failing one day. Your ideal response would be "even if God—who had never and can never fail—intends to start failing, He won't start with my case".

Then the Holy Spirit reminded me that God had covenanted Himself to the forefathers of the children of Israel and that Moses specifically had grown to his full stature in his obedience to God. These were the secrets behind the exploits of the Israelites in Egypt and their victory at the Red Sea.

> *And the LORD said unto Moses, Wherefore criest thou unto me? Speak unto the children of Isreal that they go forward; but lift thou up thy rod, and stretch out thine hand over the Sea, and divide it; and the children of Israel shall go on dry ground through the midst of the Sea. (Ex 14 vs. 15 -16)*

What a wonder to know that Moses had in his hand what God needed to rescue His dear people! How amazing to know that God did not send an angel to part the sea for His people! Moses had the rod in his hand but knew nothing much about the rod aside what it was used for in pharaoh's palace—where the rod turned into a snake.

When we grumble, complain and become depressed in the face of challenges, we only have to look around, as we have in our care, in our house, in our hands, in our minds, in our communities and in our neighbourhoods, those things that are required to move us on to our destiny without knowing we have them. Again, what we fail to do on most occasions was what Moses did: cry unto the LORD for Help.

God is not a supermarket

We have our targets already thought out and we just tell God as if He should pick up His jotter and pen our orders and conditions which He must execute within a particular time frame. I have heard people pray in churches and confess to God about other the gods they have left to come to Him. They remind Him of how those gods acted and responded fast as if to mean that they had done God a favour by calling on Him, as if He is their servant and should deliver what they want at their own stipulated time, otherwise they would return to 'faster' gods and God will lose their patronage. The Holy Spirit made it clear that Moses' prayer was not an order or command from Moses to God.

Is it not another wonder when God said, "speak unto the children of Israel that they go forward". How could He had given this order before the words in verse 16? If the children of Israel heard Moses charge them to push forward, seeing the sea ahead, would they not question Moses' sanity? But God knew what he was doing. He acts *only* according to His timing and *only* for His glory.

> *And Moses stretched out his hand over the Sea, and the Lord caused the Sea to go back by a strong east wind all that night, and made the Sea dry land, and the waters were divided. And the children of Israel went into the midst of the Sea upon the dry ground; and the waters were a wall unto them on their right hand, and on their left ... And the waters returned and covered the chariots, and the horsemen, and all the host of Pharaoh that came into the Sea after them, there remained not so much as one of them.* (Ex 14 vs. 21- 22, 28 KJV)

God came into the picture to do what no scientific prowess has ever replicated and will ever replicate. The strong wind which blew to make a 12-mile-path through the Red Sea and to hold the waters up like a hill 75-100 ft high was strong enough to blow all the Israelites and the Egyptians away. The waters were frozen solid on both sides as the Israelites walked through the Red Sea.

It must have been rare and amazing to the children of Israel as they saw what God did in such a short time, and how He gave them the pillar of fire as light to them and beclouded the Egyptians with darkness. I have often imagined what could children of Israel been thinking as they passed through 12 miles of dry ground in the Red Sea. I tried to imagine how the Israelites felt seeing pharaoh and his men die, without any of the Israelites getting injured or dying in the process. What a great thing to be on the winning side! In Ex 14 vs. 30, the Bible says:

> *Thus the LORD saved Israel that day out of the hand of the Egyptians; and Israel saw the Egyptians dead upon the Sea shore.*

In whatever dilemma or problem you find yourself, even when it is human to be cowardly or afraid, it is then that you should be the most courageous. Even when God's words seem to be a suicide command—when He says "go forward" and the Red Sea is what is ahead of you and the pharaoh's army has sent out your death warrant—that is when you need to be the most confident, not in yourself, not in any human or scientific strength, not in your company or wealth, not in your eloquence or wisdom, but in the God, whose YEA is AMEN.

Chapter 2

The Death of Jesus' Friend

Many people in the scriptures have passed through terrible challenges despite being God's generals. For instance, Job had his fair share and in an instance he said,

> "But he knows where I am and what I've done. He can cross-examine me all he wants, and I'll pass the test for honours."
> (Job 23 vs. 10 TMB).

This means he, like others, knew God permitted his tribulations yet he refused to revoke his allegiance to God.

Like the case cited in chapter one, this chapter will review the events in John 11. Having read this Bible passage over and over, I had mixed feelings. It is great to read that Jesus had friends with whom He had a personal commitment. It is great to read that my Saviour could be as emotional as human being. I am equally glad to read the conversation between Jesus and Martha, which was a product of an intimate relationship. But I became sober knowing that my Lord's friend died and worse still he had to delay His trip to Lazarus' place by two days. We shall therefore review, here, some verses from this long chapter to unearth the teachings of the Holy Spirit.

When the Going Was Good

> *There they made him a supper, and Martha served, but Lazarus was one of them that sat at the table with him. Then took Mary a pound of ointment of Spikenard, very costly, and anointed the feet of Jesus, and wiped his feet with her hair: and the house was filled with the odour of the ointment... then said Jesus, let her alone: against the day of my burying hath she kept this.* (John 12 vs. 2-3, 7 KJV)

The above verses will serve as the building blocks for the issues we shall review. The event in these verses was recorded after the John 11 events, but when I considered the event along with Luke 10 vs. 38-42, I concluded that Mary and Martha did not start to relate with Jesus just after the demise of their brother, Lazarus. They had been Jesus' students long before their brother passed away. Mary had preferred to sit at Jesus' feet while learning and to wipe them with her hair after anointing Jesus with the costly ointment of spikenard. The conversation between Jesus and Martha reveals the extent of their friendship with the rabbi, and inviting Jesus to supper in their house offers insights on their intimate relationship with the Master. I got to discover how important these people were to Jesus:

- Their house was one of the few places Jesus ate with others and He did so on two occasions (LK 10 vs. 38-42, John 12 vs. 2-8);
- They were privileged to have had a significant supper with Christ; Jesus had three suppers in His last seven days and this was the first;
- The anointing of Jesus here was one of the two anointings Jesus had in His last seven days.

They must have offered Jesus the best meals they were able to afford on those two occasions and scriptures revealed that the oil Mary anointed Jesus with was *very costly* (KJV), *very expensive* (TMB, AMP), *of great price* (DBY), *of great value* (BBE), and *very precious* (ASV). In short, they were Jesus' friends when the going was good. They did not hold back their hospitality, their wealth and their hearts from their rabbi friend. The understanding of their relationship with the Lord when all was well with them will offer a good foundation as we review their situation during the grievous moments.

Sickness and the Death of Jesus' Friend

> *Now a certain man was sick, named Lazarus, of Bethany, the town of Mary and her sister Martha. It was that Mary which anointed the Lord with ointment, and wiped his feet with her hair, whose brother*

> *Lazarus was sick. Therefore his sisters sent unto him saying, Lord, behold, he whom thou lovest is sick.* (John 11, vs. 1-3 KJV)

The first thing to note here is that this is one of the very few cases where status, condition, failure or otherwise of men were mentioned before their names. It was the same in the case of Mephiboseth in II Sam 4 vs. 4, where "lame" was mentioned twice before his name. Likewise, in the case of Nabal (I Sam 25 vs. 2-3), his personality, character strength and weaknesses were men-tioned before his name was. But what is more significant in this context was that the sickness of Lazarus carried more weight in the passage.

It was that Mary . . . is another phrase that got my attention. Of course there were many women in the Bible with this name, so it became necessary for John to describe which of them. And the event in John 12 vs. 3-8, was what seemed best to John to use as a descriptive example to distinguish this woman from other women. I found it necessary to add that the event in John 12 vs. 3 being mentioned here does not necessarily follow as taking place before the death of Lazarus. Lazarus had died beforehand. It only happened that John was writing the epistle some years after the whole scenario had taken place. It is amazing to know that a long chapter had to be built around the goodwill of Mary's unparalleled relationship with her rabbi. It seems that John must have definitely thought it wise to use Mary's place as the foundation on which the scenario should be built.

Lord, behold, he whom thou lovest is sick Is another great statement from Mary that caught my attention. Mary did not just send a message to Jesus; she sent an emotional one. She communicated Lazarus' condition to Jesus.

Sir, your good friend is very very sick (TLB)

Master, he whom you hold dear is ill (WNT)

Master, see who you hold dear is ill (MNT)

Lord, your dear friend is ill (BBE)

Sir, lo, he whom thou dost love is ailing (YLT)

Lord, he whom you love [so well] is sick (AMP)

Lord, the one you love is sick (NIV)

Master, the one you love so very much is sick (TMB)

Lord, behold, he for whom you have great affection is sick (WEB)

Above are different renditions of Mary's message to Jesus during Lazarus' sickness. Through endearing words such as *love, dear, friend,* and *affection,* Mary showed that she knew and believed Jesus' love for Lazarus and she did not send the message as "Lord, my brother Lazarus is sick", or as "Lord, Lazarus is sick."

She removed herself and Martha from the entire picture. To her, their being Lazarus' sisters was not enough of a basis to bring Jesus into action; rather, His being Lazarus' beloved friend.

Her message was built on the Lord Jesus/Lazarus, love (bond), and *sick* (the reason for the call). In other circumstances, we could see people create a message about themselves, and little or none about God. Her message was complete and perfect. I took notice of the word "love" which is the bond between Jesus and Lazarus. Mary knew what Jesus would do for whom He had great affection, and for whom He loves, and she built her message around that bond. *Sick* in this context was not the first in Mary's message, but the last. She did not ask Jesus to come straight away to do anything but only to inform Him. Yet it was with reference to the bond and the names it connects together.

Mary's choice of words in the message she sent to Jesus, is far from what we would see today. While others will see her message as an incomplete prayer, I see it as a perfect one. Theologians have observed that she did not add what she actually desired that Jesus do. She did not need to do that, as she knew what Jesus was capable of doing, especially for the one He loved. And that Jesus eventually fulfilled her expectations is enough proof to refute the argument that her prayer was an incomplete.

Imagining the mind set of Martha, as we shall soon discover, explains Martha and Mary's level of

The Death of Jesus' Friend

faith—they did not need to dictate or order Jesus into action before He acted. This occasion is one of the few places in the Bible where Jesus did not ask what the beneficiaries of His miracles wanted Him to do before He acted. Definitely, we can assume it was because Jesus knew the situation.

These were not the others like Bartholomew; not like the man at the bank of Bethesda river; not Jarius; not the centurion; not the widow whose son died; not the Samaritan woman or the lepers. These were Jesus' friends, and more still, Lazarus, Jesus' dear and good friend whom He loved and had great affection for. Mary, having good knowledge of all these, needed not to make her request the way those lepers made theirs. She needed not to shout the way Bartholomew did; and needed not to sorrow the way the widow did. Jesus, for her, was not the miracle worker but a FRIEND. And she constructed her message as such—not as to the Healer but as to the Friend who cared so much.

As I continued to wonder at the level of Mary's intimacy with Jesus, I came to understand that she built her message and friendship on their bond of love with Jesus. If we excise "lovest" from her words—of prayers, the remaining words would be incomplete. In essence, her confidence and the type of request she made can only be possible and effective when there is a bond in place. This bond not having been established was why some had to come in through the roof to access Jesus; climb a tree to behold Him pass; shout to get His attention and weep to catch His emotions.

But *"Mary hath chosen that good part, which shall not be taken away from her"* (LK 10 vs. 42 KJV). Not even the death of Lazarus could take away the good part and the friendship that Mary had with Jesus. I must then mention that she did not choose the good part in the middle of her crisis and sorrow. She chose the good part when the going was good. The path she chose paid off as her prayer resulted in an undeniable miracle. A prayer then can be defined as "any message that is capable of bringing God's hands into action and for His own glory alone."

The Bonding Before the Sickness

For anyone to pray in the words of Mary and expect a response without a bond with the Lord will be like a farmer aiming to harvest maize without first securing a plot as farmland as well as sowing it. The bond is the ground on which the friendship would grow. It is therefore a necessity for one to have Christ in one's life for one to be capable of relying on Christ to help in times of trouble. It should not to be an attempt at getting Him to do what we want during emergencies as we often do, but a procedure that must take place and that will cause our prayers to be answered when emergencies arise.

For you to bring His hands into action, you must first secure a bond between the two of you and the only way to do this, is for you to accept Him and offer Him a place in your life **at the moment** when everything is well with you. Having Jesus, to Mary, was an insurance scheme. She was committed and devoted to the friendship when everything was peaceful around her and her refuge functional when her brother got sick. Moreover, it was not a bond just between Mary and Jesus, but between Jesus and *he whom thou lovest.* This implies that there was equally a bond between Jesus and Lazarus. Lazarus too, had been Jesus' friend, just like Mary when the going was very good. Why not take Him into your life now? I have the pleasure of telling you that He will not only be there as your insurance cover when problems arise, but also when you get to eternity.

The Irony of Jesus' Love

>*Now Jesus loved Martha, and her sister and Lazarus. When he had heard therefore that he was sick, he abode two days still in the same place where he was* (vs. 5-6 KJV).

>*Although Jesus was very fond of Martha, Mary, Lazarus, he stayed where he was for the next two days and made no move to go to them.* (TLB)

>*Jesus loved Martha and her sister and Lazarus, but oddly, when he heard that Lazarus was sick, he stayed on where he was for two more days.* (TMB)

What an irony of Jesus' love! I wondered as I read these verses again and again. I expected Jesus to leave where He was with immediate effect and travel towards Bethany to heal Lazarus. Peradventure he was very far away or busy where He was. I expected to read about the rabbi sending forth His powerful words instantly to heal his good and dear friend. I expected to read about Jesus coming into the picture to alleviate his friend's pains and usher in the comfort that good health offers. But my Lord did not leave where He was for another two days. It was exciting seeing the word "oddly" in TMB version of vs. 6. What would He have done to the one "He does not love" if He had to tarry for two days where He was before coming to attend to the one he loved? Is that ever a true love? These are questions that ravaged my heart as I studied this passage for the first time as a child. Because the children's church teacher wanted to keep us in suspense, he did not immediately teach us the latter part. When I came to understand the events that followed this, I asked again, "Why did He delay?" The purpose why he delayed going to Mary and Martha and other issues in the chapter will be discussed later. However, I was glad to again discover that Jesus was monitoring Lazarus' condition although He stayed away for two days.

> *These things said he: and after that he saith unto them, our friend Lazarus sleepeth; but I go that I may awake him out of sleep. Then said his disciples, Lord, if he sleep, he shall do well. Then said Jesus*

unto them plainly, Lazarus is dead.' (vs. 11-12, 14 KJV)

He did not leave where he was for two days until He discovered that Lazarus was dead. He seemed slow but He intentionally delayed His actions. It was great to know that Lazarus was not only addressed as Jesus' friend by Mary; Jesus himself called him "Our friend". But I became puzzled that the rest of the "our" team, which were the disciples, did not remind Jesus of Lazarus' condition during the two days.

As seen in vs. 16, Thomas saw it as a deadly adventure for Jesus to go near Jerusalem because of those who had attempted stoning Him (*vs. 7-8*). Could they not have solicited Christ's words to settle Lazarus' sickness if they were afraid of the risk in the trip? Jesus called Lazarus His friend but He resided two days longer in the place where He was. If He delayed the healing of His friend, it is important to know that it is not enough to just be His friend, but to understand His timing.

That He did not go immediately does not take away the truth that Lazarus was Jesus' friend. When He seems not to be coming into your situation as fast as you would expect or as immediate as the circumstance demands, let your understanding of Him be strong and do not lose your confidence in Him. It is important you understand where He is at every time. How did Mary know where Jesus was that she sent the messenger to meet Him there? She had the "diary and agenda" of the Spirit-led-Christ in her heart. Perhaps that made it possible for her to locate Jesus and not running from mountain to mountain. Whatever the degree of the oddity that loving Him poses, your decision to stay your faith in Him will count on important days.

When He Seems Late

> *Then when Jesus came, he found that he had lain in the grave four days already. (vs. 17 KJV)*

With Bethany just about fifteen furlongs—about two miles—off Jerusalem, we could assume that Lazarus died the day the message was sent. If it took the messenger a day to journey to Jesus, and Jesus stayed two days and took a day to journey to Bethany, then we could safely assume that Lazarus died perhaps before the messenger got to Jesus. My Lord could have seen the picture of Lazarus on the sick bed before Mary's message was sent. That the message did not spur Him to leave immediately it only showed that the omniscient and omnipotent rabbi was intentional.

> *Then Martha, as soon as she heard that Jesus was coming, went and met him: but Mary sat still in the house. (vs. 20)*

Not minding whether His arrival was too late, Martha ran out of the house to meet her rabbi. Lazarus, dead or alive, her friendship with the Master remained intact. Although Mary tarried in the house, it was definitely not because she had lost confidence in her teacher—someone had to remain in the house with the sympathisers. This raises a serious question: How many of the so-called believers of this age would still run out to meet Jesus, seeing He arrived four days after the burial of the Lazerus?

Knowledge Precedes Belief

The Conversation between Jesus and Martha

> *Then said Martha unto Jesus, Lord, if thou hast been here, my brother had not died. But I know, that even now, whatsoever thou wilt ask of God, God will give it thee. Jesus said unto her, thy brother shall rise again. Martha saith unto him, I know that he shall rise again in the resurrection at the last day. Jesus said unto her, I am the resurrection, and the life; he that believeth in me, though he were dead, yet shall he live: And whosoever liveth and believeth in me shall never die. Believe thou this? She saith unto him, Yea, Lord: I believe that thou art the Christ, the son of God, which should come into the world. (vs. 21-27 KJV)*

> *"Yes, master", she replied; I thoroughly believe that you are the Christ, the son of God who was to come into the world. (vs. 27 WNT)*

> *Believest thou this? She saith to him; yes sir, I have believed that thou art the Christ, the son of God, who is coming to the world. (vs. 27 YLT)*
>
> *Yes, Master, all along I have believed that you are the Messiah, the son of God who comes into the world. (vs. 27 TMB)*

From the various conversations between Jesus and his disciples, the breath-catching conversations in the verses above, which contain great lessons for believers, stand out. Martha did not allow the grief caused by the death of her dear brother to mask her knowledge of the Master. She knew the closeness between Jesus and God, and that Jesus could cause God to work miracles at any time, however seemingly late. Not just that, she knew that 'then' was not late for Jesus to display His almighty power. Martha mentioned resurrection even though Jesus had not taken them through the class on it, save a brief mention in *John 2 vs. 19* and *5 vs. 29*.

In essence, Martha must have gained her knowledge on the resurrection subject during one of those private sessions of teaching they had with Him. She knew two significant things: that whatsoever Jesus wanted would be granted Him by God, and that there shall be the resurrection of the dead on the last day. These formed the basis for her faith to thrive. She did not venture into seeking knowledge when the need arose; she had gotten the necessary knowledge before the demand arose. She did not, in any wise, question the power and might of Jesus, and did not ask what delayed Him. By expressing her belief, she validated her knowledge of Christ and of Christ's link with God.

It would be mere fiction to express belief in someone you do not know: Knowledge precedes belief. The knowledge-belief component of our faith does not come overnight or during emergencies, but over time as we build trust, conviction and confidence in the party to be believed. Martha had immersed herself in Jesus' teachings, and had taken time to understand Jesus' impartations. Consequently, this knowledge became a crucial asset in her belief in Jesus.

WNT and TMB offer words I so much admire: such as 'thoroughly', and 'believed'. *Thoroughly* means without reservation, entirely, completely. YLT uses the word *believed* which means that she was not just trying to believe, but she had total faith in Jesus.

> *And when she had so said, she went her way and called Mary her sister secretly, saying, the master is come, and called for thee .... Then when Mary was come where Jesus was, and saw him, she fell down at his feet, saying unto him, Lord, if thou hadst been here, my brother had not died (vs. 28, 32 KJV).*

Mary most likely was not aware that Christ had been around before Martha came in to inform her (*vs. 28*). Her quick rising (*jumped up and ran out ... TMB*) could only explain that she would never have remained indoors had she known.

Mary was very close to Jesus, she learnt at His feet (*Lk 10 vs. 38.42*); she anointed Him and wiped His feet with her hair (*John 12 vs. 3*); and when the time of grief came, the feet of Jesus again became where she mourned. Thus, *John 11 vs 32* raises another question: Neither Mary nor Martha wept until Jesus' arrival, perhaps because they imagined Lazarus would still be alive if Jesus had come earlier. And Mary expressed the same confidence in Christ, as Martha—not uncertain, but very sure that Lazarus would never had died in the presence of the Messiah. Like Martha, Mary had also built her knowledge in Christ before the need arose.

The coping mechanisms of great men in their times of grief are built and maintained when all is well with them.

Where Have Ye Laid Him?

> *When Jesus therefore saw her weeping, and the Jews also weeping which came with her, he groaned in the spirit, and was troubled, and said, where have ye laid him? They said unto him, Lord, come and see. Jesus wept. Then said the Jews, Behold how he loved him! And some of them said, could not this man, which opened the eyes of the blind, have caused that even this man should not have died?"*
>
> *Jesus therefore again groaning in himself*

> *cometh to the grave. It was a cave, and a stone lay upon it. (vs. 33-38 KJV)*

Three things must have prompted Jesus into action here. It must be said, however, that had the three things not happened at all (as He had said earlier), He would have gone ahead to perform this miracle. First, it was not a palatable thing for Jesus to behold his favourite student, Mary, shed tears—he groaned and was troubled in the spirit about this.

Second, seeing His friend placed in the cave and a mighty stone rolled across the entry, made Jesus weep. This verse shows the sympathy Jesus had for His friends. He wept with those who wept to the extent that even His enemies acknowledged His love and compassion.

Third, in addition to the crowd acknowledging Jesus' grief and sadness, they also questioned His power and His love for his friends. They thought He could have prevented Lazarus from dying in the first place, as nobody imagined Him raising Lazarus up from the dead.

> *Jesus said, take ye away the stone. Martha, the sister of him that was dead, saith unto him, Lord, by this time he stinketh: for he hath been dead four days. Jesus saith unto her, said I not unto thee, that, if thou wouldest believe, thou shouldest see the glory of God. (vs. 39-40 KJV)*

Martha's response was not out of place. Only Jesus knew from the beginning what He must set about to do. To avoid the embarrassment that the putrefactive odour and emotional stress might pose, Martha suggested that Jesus should let the "sleeping Lazarus lie". She had resolved in her mind to see Lazarus again at the resurrection of the saints, not as a mortal being. This was the second time in the passage that her faith did not match Jesus' expectations completely—first was in *vs. 24-25*. Jesus told Martha that her brother was going to live again '***now***.' Martha answered "yes" (only to postpone Lazarus' rising on the last day). And here, four days seemed long enough for Martha to conclude it would be impossible for Jesus to raise Lazarus up. Perhaps, she believed that Jesus could raise the dead *if still fresh*, or unburied or dead for less than four days.

Regardless whether her belief was great enough or not, there was no record of Martha arguing with Jesus. She knew that nothing was impossible or difficult for the Lord. On the two occasions when Jesus gave the next reassuring sentence, Martha submitted completely.

Among the several crises rocking the early followers of Christ, the paramount one was a lack of faith or unbelief—praying as if unto a powerless God who cannot answer. They lacked a true bond with God. Indeed, this crisis exists today and must be addressed for the church to once again be effective like the early church. When many of us pray, we "challenge" God.

The Death of Jesus' Friend

These exemplary sisters did not question Jesus; they asked all their questions during those classes. They did not argue with Him, and did not hesitate in applying all they had learnt from Him.

"Unwrap Him and Let Him Go!"

> *Then they took away the stone from the place where the dead was laid. And Jesus lifted up his eyes, and said, Father, I thank thee that thou hast heard me.*
>
> *And I knew that thou hearest me always: but because of the people which standby I said it, that they may believe that thou hast sent me. And when he thus had spoken, he cried with a loud voice, "Lazarus, come forth". And he that was dead came forth, bound hand and foot with grave clothes; and his face was bound about with a napkin. Jesus saith unto them, "loose him, and let him go". (vs. 41-44)*

The stone that was used to cover the tomb of Lazarus was rolled aside at the command of Jesus. For a single stone to be used to cover a tomb, the said stone must have been very big to the extent that a set of people, was requested to perform the task. Next was the prayer of my Lord. Only the prayer in *John 17* is longer in content than what Jesus prayed at the grave side of

Lazarus—of all Jesus' prayers. Note that the Lord did not challenge God into action. He started by giving thanks to the Father for previous answers, and that He was sure God heard him always.

It must be pointed out that when we pray now, we violate the protocol of appreciating the omnipotent, omniscient attributes of God. We have all the reasons in the world to defend our emergency prayers. We seem to have been born to ask all the time, but forget to thank God for the last package we took away. Instead of updating our ways of appreciating this awesome God, we update our manner of asking and reasons for asking, as if God created us to be at our service.

Jesus went ahead to state the purpose why Lazarus had to die. And He cried with a loud voice, now not unto God, but unto the dead. At this juncture, I became puzzled that Lazarus who had stopped breathing came to life when Life came to the grave-side and made the ears of the dead active. Hearing became possible for the man that had been dead for four days and had been buried. It is not stated in the passage that Jesus repeated the statement, or that He touched Lazarus' body: He only spoke once. The Bible says:

> *The dead man came out (RSV); And out walked the man who had been dead (AMP).*

The dead man heard and walked out of the tomb. It was not stated in the passage that Lazarus was helped out of the tomb—he came out. At the hearing of Jesus' words, there was nothing that remained dead in

The Death of Jesus' Friend

Lazarus' body. Jesus, therefore, commanded that all the grave clothing that had been used to bury Lazarus be removed. He wanted His friend to be free of everything connected to death as He commanded:

> *Loose him, and let him go (KJV).*
>
> *Unwrap him and let him go. (TLB)*
>
> *Make him free and let him go. (BBE)*
>
> *Free him and let him go. (WEB)*

What cuts across most versions concerning Jesus' order here is *'go'*. When He got to the tomb, He brought life to the dead. He did not just raise up the dead; He also set him free. He imparted into him all that was needed for him to go. As I studied the latter part of the chapter, I was able to discover what Jesus wanted Lazarus to go and do. He wanted his friend to go and represent what the power of God could do. He wanted His friend to go and enjoy life in its fullness; to go and be dead no more; to go and show the unbelievers what was missing in their lives.

I have all the confidence within me that if you also would bring into your life the bond that existed between Jesus and His friends, take the time to study and acquire knowledge about Him, believe in Him alone and commit your entirety to Him, then you can also enjoy more than Lazarus did. Even if your case seems to be a different version of death, the message here is that God's love can bring life into the dead parts of you. And one important thing that you must understand is that because we are Christians does not guarantee immunity to us from the challenges and trials of life.

Being a Christian the promise of eternal life and fellowship with the Father is guaranteed. Eternal life might come after some troublesome times in this terrestrial place, but the important thing is that we have a place with the Father on the last day. Again, as much as possible, we enjoy the goodness of our salvation here on earth.

Take note and remember, that if the great men and women in the Bible and God's favourite generals, had to pass through trials and tribulations, and if His people faced the brink of disaster between the pharaoh and the Red Sea, then whosoever is preaching that a Christian must not henceforth encounter challenges is only preaching heresies. Jesus himself said that we shall face challenges, but if we take to heart Jesus' teachings, no challenge is too great.

Chapter 3

Abraham's Time of Life

> *Now the Lord had said unto Abram, get thee out of thy country, and from thy kindred, and from thy father's house, unto a land that I will shew thee; and I will make thee a great nation and I will bless thee, and make thy name great; and thou shall be a blessing.... So Abram departed, as the Lord had spoken unto him, and Lot went with him; and Abram was seventy and five years old when he departed out of Haran. (Gen 12 vs. 1-4 KJV)*

The latter part of *Gen 11* reveals the family history of Terah. What caught my attention was that Terah died in Haran. He did not get to his destination though the Bible does not provide too many details about his plight and status in Haran.

Terah and his family were given to idolatry prior to the event in *Gen 11 vs. 31-32*. It seems likely that after he was converted from idolatry in Ur of the Chaldees, he departed for Canaan, perhaps in an attempt to flee his sinful lifestyle there and the persecution from his people (*Acts 7vs. 2*).

God's initial step was to get Abraham out of idol worship in Ur. The Bible does not say too much about Abraham's lifestyle while in the land of Ur. But his heeding God's call without any form of resistance suggests that he was probably a seeker of God before this passage. He left Ur with Terah, his father, and the length of time they spent in Haran was not specifically recorded. However, Terah's death in Haran did not stop Abraham from realising the target his father could not pursue successfully. What is most amazing is that he never worried about losing those important acquaintances, properties, connections, family history and, more importantly, not knowing where his destination lies. He obeyed God's word and left.

> *...and into the land of Canaan they came.*
> *(Gen 12 vs. 5)*

It must be stressed that Abraham did not arrive in Canaan alone; he came with his share of inheritance that he got after Terah's death as well as the converts he made in Haran who wanted to go along with him to share in the blessings God had promised him. Further reviews reveal that there were many slaves among them, at least 318 trained soldiers with their families. These 318 trained soldiers were reported to have been born in Abraham's house to 636 parents who, no doubt, had other children.

The greatness of any individual is a function of certain conditions and his/her efforts will never know success if they are not in accordance with those outlined conditions. Consider how Abraham would never have realised the covenant of God for him had he not departed the land of Ur. *Gen 12 vs. 1-4* informs me that God put those great promises across based on difficult conditions which if not obeyed would not have allowed Abraham to become great. That is God for you! All the 48 promises given to Abraham were attached to certain conditions. Self-denial, persecution, endurance and journeying by faith were all part of the package that I refer to as the *obedience* upon which Abraham's blessings were hung. "*And I will make thee ... and I will bless thee*" were given after certain "hard orders".

Even though not much information was provided about Abraham's life before his 75th year, chances are that he had commenced building his lasting relationship with God over many years. It was thought that his promised greatness would be realised in Canaan, but God began to fulfill His words concerning Abraham right from his period in Haran (*Gen 12 vs. 5*). He was an obedient follower. This means that no greatness is too hard for you to attain if only you decide to be obedient. As part of his obedience, he had to leave his father's land which meant separation. This separation helped him to avoid further distractions and pressures from the idolatrous people of Ur, which could have strangled his faith in God.

The number of years Terah spent in Haran, the reasons why Terah did not get to Canaan and the number of years it took Abraham to get to Canaan after

Terah's demise are not explicitly stated in the Bible. However, something which caught my attention was the family's history of infertility. When a woman is identified as "barren" in the Old Testament, you can depend on God to reverse it.[1]

Long before I got to know much about Terah, the Holy Spirit made me know about the infertility his marriage had to endure and how it did not stop on Abraham and Sarah's marriage (Gen. 11 vs. 30; 21 vs. 1-2), but was also passed to the unions of Isaac and Rebecca (Gen. 25 vs. 21), and, Jacob and Rachel (Gen. 29 vs. 31; 30 vs. 22).

> *And Nahor lived nine and twenty years, and begat Terah ... . And Terah lived seventy years, and begat Abram, Nahor and Haran. (Gen 12 vs. 24-26 KJV)*

Nahor gave birth to Terah when she was just 29 years old but Terah did not have a child until he was 70. In essence, the history of infertility started with Terah and he had Abraham when he was 130 years.

Having separated himself from his people and idolatry, why did God allow Terah to go through those challenges? Terah did not have any children for many years and while he was still alive, Haran his son died—perhaps soon after giving birth to Lot. My fear is that perhaps the meaning of his name, *wandering*, was

---

[1] Five Barren Women in the Old Testament|Unto Him. see: https://mitchchase.wordpress.com/2016/01 (accessed on 10 February 2019).

responsible for his failure to enter Canaan—if we could so assume.

Could Terah be facing these challenges because he or his fathers had sinned? It appears that although binding oneself unto God may bring the best out of one's destiny, yet to assume it is the end of challenges is a great misconception. Not many people knew much about Terah's conversion and obedience to depart the land of idolatry. But I found out that he must have experienced a great deal of rejection in order to follow his God. Let's assume God had intended to try His people, should it be with barrenness? What was responsible for that of Terah and four subsequent generations?

One thing I must add here is that regardless of how successful the unbelievers become while here on earth and how hard things become for believers after separation unto God and obedience to His commands, let it be known that the glory believers have by obeying God will outlast the unbelievers and span across many generations. This was what God revealed in

> *Gen 15: After these things the word of the Lord came unto Abram in a vision, saying, fear not, Abram: I am thy shield and thy exceeding great reward. (Gen 15 vs. 1 KJV)*

The peak of any man's destiny is to receive these words from God Himself. But I must remind you that obeying God's words is very essential. After a few years of Bible study, I keep asking why God would prefer to exalt the younger at the expense of the elder. Right from the first siblings in Bible history, the younger had been preferred by God. Except in the cases of the children of promise and the ones born after long waiting, all other great men in the Bible were either last born or one before the last in their clan. For example, God chose Abel over Cain, Jacob over Esau, Manasseh over Ephraim and Jacob over Esau.

However, these preferred young ones were separated, committed and loyal to God. They were found faithful while their elders weighed far less than required. David's case offers another example, as God said, "for I have rejected him" concerning David's elder brothers. I must stress here that parents of this age need to prayerfully and by every means possible assist their 'first borns'.

This mystery also worked in Abraham's favour. Terah had Haran at 70 and Abraham 60 years later but God preferred the younger and entered into a covenant with him. To explain God's choice of Abraham, Lot's lifestyle and his love for Sodom offer an idea on who Haran was. Nahor's stay in idolatrous Ur of Chaldees also validates the conclusion that Abraham was the only person that made himself available for God to use.

> *And the Lord said unto Abram, after that Lot was separated from him, lift up now thine eyes and look from the place where thou art northward, and southward, and eastward and westward: for all the land*

Abraham's Time of Life

> *which thou seest, to thee will I give it, and to thy seed forever. (Gen 13 vs. 14-15 KJV)*

After the encounter with God in *Gen 12 vs. 1-8*, he went through challenging periods. He had issues with the pharaoh where our father of faith lied. Of importance here was his deteriorating relationship with Lot. They had wealth, animals and servants but the meaning of Lot, *veil*, posed a major hindrance to Abraham's progress. Just coming out of Egypt's ordeal, Lot's servants became another issue. Abraham therefore initiated a plan that I refer to as "destiny liberating" as he requested that Lot should separate himself. Lot agreed and the Bible does not give any record of him hesitating to leave his uncle. Then, God spoke to Abraham. I found some astounding revelations in *Gen 13 vs. 14: ...after that Lot was separated from him....*

It is necessary for any man who is ready to pursue his destiny to give up certain relationships. Although Abraham had maintained a good relationship with Lot before this time, the destiny of Abraham got to a point where Lot needed to go. That those friends are there for you now does not mean they are going to be relevant to your entire course. It is necessary, however, that you do not in any way excuse these relationships. You must be very conscious and cautious of the future. Abraham's approach will be of help to you if you find the need to take the same step. You will not grow to your potential and strength if you have to settle quarrels and amend differences when you should spend that same time to realize your destiny. If you discover that a good relationship with a friend, relation or colleague at work is now being replaced with frequent quarrels and disagreements, a break from such a relationship might bring your destiny back on track.

...lift up now thine eyes....

After Lot had gone, the next stage was *lift up now thine eyes*. *Now* suggests that Abraham had been unable to communicate with others before this time because Lot, the veil, was with him. But with the veil now lifted, it became easier for Abraham to see again.

Friends, your sight determines your height! If you cannot see well, you certainly cannot go far in life. It then becomes necessary for you to identify those things that veil your eyes—those relationships and commitments that blur your sight. The eyes are not only the light of the body; they are also important to one's progress. You must be prepared to do without some 'Lots', otherwise you will have 'lots' of woes.

...and look from the place where thou art...

What a discovery! Abraham had eyes all along but they had been veiled. He had been in the right place for the fulfilment of his destiny, but he 'knew it not'. Abraham did not need to run helter-skelter; he only needed to be separated from Lot for him to be unveiled and to behold his great destiny. Wherever you find yourself, you must ensure you get God's network signals. And where you cannot get His signals, examine your relationship and partnerships; go for a refraction test to determine if your eyes are seeing well. The necessary visual acuity here is not done in an ophthalmologist's clinic but in God's clinic.

Lot's departure ushered in great promises for Abraham as well as the encounter which marked out the rest of his life. Studying *Gen 19 vs. 1-38* helped me understand that Abraham's destiny could have been veiled up forever had he not taken the deliberate step to go alone rather than retain relations that would take away his relevance.

The right and privilege of age did not affect Abraham as he allowed Lot to choose first. Parting ways with some old time friends or relations might be very hard, but if you believe that they are standing between you and God, preventing you from your destiny, please do not hesitate to let go. Do not get me wrong. I am not saying you should not keep friends and relations; even Jesus called Himself our friend, just as the Bible described Him as our brother. However, any destiny-marring relationship must be sacrificed with wisdom for you to forge ahead to your destiny.

> *And when Abram was ninety years old and nine, the Lord appeared to Abram, and said unto him, I am the Almighty God; walk before me, and be thou perfect. (Gen 17 vs. 1 KJV)*

After the events in *Genesis 13* where Abraham separated himself from Lot, seeing became an easy thing. In *Gen 15 vs. 6*, the Bible says concerning

Abraham: *And he believed in the Lord, and he counted it to him for righteousness.*

This implies that it becomes easier to believe God when one sees properly. Abraham's faith in the word of God both endeared him to God and strengthened his relationship with God. Furthermore, in *Gen 17 vs. 1*, *appeared* suggests that God revealed Himself to Abraham more than before. I must confess that I count this verse as one of the many odd verses in the Bible. The first time I studied this verse, many questions flooded my mind. I saw God as too demanding. I remember I wanted to know what God wanted from Abraham who did not compromise despite the yet-to-be-fulfilled promises. I later found answers to those questions in *Gen 15 vs. 1; Heb 6 vs. 12; Heb 11 vs. 8-10* as I grew in faith.

> *And I will make my covenant between me and thee, and will multiply thee exceedingly. (Gen 17 vs. 2 KJV)*

The demand I regarded as odd in *Gen 17 vs. 1* was then followed by great promises in *vs. 2*, where God committed Himself to His loyal servant. The appearance of the word *exceedingly* caught my attention. Mentioned earlier in *Gen 15 vs. 1*, I discovered that *exceedingly*, used to describe great reward and fruitfulness, became rare after Abraham's days (*Gen 16 vs. 10, 17 vs. 20*). But before God committed Himself this much, Abraham had been amazingly loyal in the

Abraham's Time of Life

face of Sarah's barrenness and delayed fulfilment of God's words.

The word *exceeding(ly)* as seen in *Gen 15 vs. 1; 16 vs. 10; 17 vs. 2, 6,* and *20* was used to describe multiple blessings, fruitful endeavours and great rewards. With the way the word was deployed, the Holy Spirit made me understand that exceeding fruitfulness, multiplication of blessings and great rewards must be preceded by rarely palatable circumstances—much like going through a refinery—which will prove the bearers of such blessings worthy of them. Although only a few can remain obedient and loyal while enduring afflictions as father Abraham was, I understand that if any man can stick to God in the face of troubles, *exceeding* greatness will come upon the individual. I was also made to understand that God made His chosen men pass through refineries of different forms, and until they come out perfected, the glory remains "pending".

> *But he knoweth the way that I take: when he hath tried me, I shall come forth as gold. (Job 23 vs. 10 KJV)*

Even though Job did not know God's intention for all the ordeals he faced, he knew he was going through the refinery. Moses, Elijah, David, Job, Daniel, our Saviour Jesus Christ and most of the apostles were men honed by their various refinery experiences.

But what if Abraham had defaulted? Of course, the answer is straightforward! Abraham rarely interrupted God whenever they conversed except in *Gen 17 vs. 17-18*. It was likely he had concluded that the birth of Isaac was impossible. Despite this, he still remained steadfast to God's commands and instructions. Obedience, to Abraham, must continue 'regardless whether God fulfills His words or not'.

> *And Abraham said unto God, O that Ishmael might live before thee! (Gen 17 vs. 18 KJV)*

Abraham went the extra-mile believing God even when God's promises could no longer, humanly speaking, be realised. Abraham had resolved not to waver in his stand to abide by God's instructions. Otherwise, all the covenants God made would all not have come his way. Abraham's bountiful blessings that we all clamour for today were borne out of exceeding loyalty and obedience to God. Until the church of this age gets to understand this clearly, we will only continue to sing the famous "Abraham's blessings are mine" chorus without the blessings coming our way.

During the encounter in *Gen 17 vs. 1-22*, his name was changed from Abram—exalted father—to Abraham—father of a multitude. When the dawn of his time of life began to appear, Abraham's position changed from being the father of his household to being the father of nations and generations to come. All these were made possible because of Abraham's endurance and obedience to God.

Again in *vs. 2-13*, the repetition of certain words caught my attention. *And* appeared 25 times and most times where it appeared it was used to usher in another promise, covenant or reassurance. As a conjunction, it was used to combine great promises together. *Covenant* was mentioned seven times. The word *covenant* appears in the Bible 292 times, and far less than one-third of those appearances came from God's mouth. Reviews have it that God did not use the word *covenant* in his messages up to 100 times in the entire Bible. But in our study text, He used it seven times in 12 verses in a single conversation, while it was used nine times in the entire conversation (*17 vs. 1-22*).

Everlasting covenant is one of those expressions scarcely used by God in the Bible. It is not just a covenant, it is a covenant that will exist as long as God and people exist. In other words, it has no end.

When *covenant* was mentioned nine times in the 22 verses alongside *Everlasting covenant*, I saw God reassuring father Abraham. These two phrases appeared together for the first time in the Bible when God was conversing with Noah in Gen 9 vs. 16, and they co-occurred for a total of 15 times in the entire Bible. Of the fifteen times, ten were from God's mouth, while Isaiah, David and Paul made mention of the other five. To add value to this conversation, the two phrases were mentioned twice in 12 verses and thrice in the whole 22 verses. What a man was Abraham!

At this level, one needs to consider the greatness of these covenants and their implications for Abraham. In pursuing this, the Holy Spirit urged me to search out two more words. *God*—represented as I, me, my, myself—was mentioned 22 times in these 12 verses. Perhaps, God did not lay emphasis on Himself this much in conversations He had with others. As if that was not enough, in a single conversation spanning 12 verses, Abraham was mentioned—as Abram, Abraham, thee, thou, thy, you—in a significant 44 times. There is no other conversation that God had with others in which he puts so much emphasis on the person He addresses. While angels interacted with Elijah and Jacob, the Holy Spirit conversed with Jesus and the Apostles. Although Isaiah, Jeremiah, Ezekiel and Moses heard Him directly, the emphasis on Himself and on the listener were not up to 22 and 44 times, respectively, in just 12 verses.

Can you take a break and ruminate on this? Conversations between friends, couples, parents and children, perhaps would not produce all these emphases. But the conversation between God and a human did. God had so much trust in Abraham that He made him His confidant (*Gen 18 vs. 17*). This unprecedented relationship is explainable, but it is one of the 'rarest achievements' in the Bible. Abraham's unreserved obedience, loyalty, and belief in God, regardless of his challenges, the delayed fulfilment of promises and age, ushered in the best relationship between God and human beings ever recorded.

Whatever problem you might be passing through now, or that you have passed through, nothing is better than your making the best use of them to enhance your relationship with Him. And one thing I have discovered about God is that the more you know Him, the more you will crave to know Him more.

Contents of the Covenant

The promises and covenants were channelled in 5 directions: Abraham, Sarah, Isaac, Ishmael (Hagar) and generations to come. Another significant part is the demands that all of them carried.

It must be noted that God called Abraham out unto Himself after He had conquered the human race, by confusing their tongues at the tower of Babel (*Gen 11 vs. 1-9*). God was starting a new order through Abraham:

- *I will make of thee a great nation (Gen 12 vs. 1-3; 13 vs. 16; 17 vs. 18 -20; 24 vs. 34, 35; Gal 3)*
- *I will make thy name great (Gen 12 vs. 1- 3; Ex 2 vs. 24, 25; 6 vs. 3-8)*
- *Thou shall be a blessing (Gen 12 vs. 1-3; Gal 3 vs. 13 -14)*
- *I will bless them that bless thee (Gen 12 vs. 1-3; Mt 25 vs. 31- 46)*
- *I will bless thee (Gen 13 vs. 14-18; 15 vs. 18-21; Gal 3)*
- *I will curse them that curse thee (Zech 14; Mt 25 vs. 31-46)*

- *In thee shall all the nations of the world be blessed (Deut 28 vs. 8-14; Isa 60 vs. 3-5; 66 vs. 18-21).*
- *And thou shall go to thy fathers in peace; thou shall be buried in a good old age (Gen 15 vs. 15).*
- *They answered and said unto him, Abraham is our father .... (John 8 vs. 39a KJV)*

This assembly of Jews in John chapter 8 were rightful heirs to the Abrahamic covenants. However, they did not know that inheritance is not based on flesh and blood alone but on salvation and righteousness. It is not enough for you to pray and request in the name of the God of Abraham simply because you consider yourself a member of his lineage. It is a necessity for you to follow after father Abraham in obedience and just living. Of course, two clauses exist in Abraham's case: first, he had the mystery of being the younger sibling in his favour and the second is that he separated himself unto God in righteous and obedient living, despite his flaws.

If you are in a tunnel, going through a refinery, having challenges and/or barrenness of any form, please believe Him, seek Him the more, pray to Him, depend only on Him, and follow Him. Even if I cannot see anything at all, I can, at least, see the dawn of your time of life come into view and approaching fast in Jesus' name.

Chapter 4

Ruth's Time of Life

Now it came to pass in the days when the judges ruled, that there was a famine in the land. And a certain man of Bethlehem-Judea went to sojourn in the country of Moab, he and his wife, and his two sons (Ruth 1 vs. 1 KJV).

The expression that starts this verse, . . . *Now it came to pass in the days,* occurs five times in the scripture. In each occurrence, it denotes an impending trouble. Although it is quite discouraging to start reviewing Ruth's time of life with this discovery, it is more reassuring to note as well that the troubles in those five instances were followed by deliverance and a happy ending. It must be noted that the transition from trouble through deliverance to a happy ending might not be achieved if there is no perseverance.

And Elimelech Naomi's husband died; and she was left, and her two sons. And they took them wives of the women of Moab; the name of the one was Orpah, and the name of the other Ruth; and they dwelled there about ten years And Mahlon and Chilion

> *died also both of them; ... (Ruth 1 vs. 3 -5a KJV)*

The trouble, as explained in verse 1, was famine as well as the decision of Elimelech, a Bethlehemite, to sojourn in the land of the Moabites. How long he lived in the country of Moab is not stated in the Bible and the cause of his probable early death was also not given. What was shocking was the death of both Mahlon and Chilion.

After the death of Elimelech, Mahlon and Chilion married in the land of the Moabites and had their marriages for only ten years. The cause of their deaths was not given in the scripture except for the Targum's explanation that it was due to their marriage to foreign women. It is not known whether they became idol worshippers in the process. It is also not recorded if both of them died on a single day. We can ascertain, however, that they died within a period of a year. This marked the peak of Naomi's troubles. She became hopeless having to part ways with her daughters-in-law.

> *Wherefore she went forth out of the place where she was, and her two daughters in law with her; and they went on the way to return unto the land of Judah. And Naomi said unto her two daughters in law, go, return each to her mother's house: the LORD deal kindly with you as ye have dealt with the dead, and with me. The*

LORD grants you that ye may find rest, each of you in the house of her husband. Then she kissed them; and they lifted up their voice and wept. (Ruth 1 vs. 7- 9 KJV)

Although Naomi left Judea with her family to survive in the land of Moab, it was after her afflictions she became aware that the famine that rocked Judea had been replaced with plenty. So she opted to return to her land and people. It can be assumed that it could have been a bearable experience for Naomi if she had gotten grandchildren from her daughters-in-law. However, it is hard to understand why Orpah and Ruth did not have children for their late husbands despite their living together for 10 years (*1 vs. 4*). It would have made sense for Orpah and Ruth to cling to Naomi had they born children for their men.

Therefore not having children made their separation from Naomi the best option. It could be deciphered from the passage that they were still relatively young and remaining childless widows for the rest of their lives would have amounted to foolishness. Naomi therefore gathered her courage and decided to face her inevitable loneliness when she charged them to return to their mothers, to start life afresh.

Furthermore, it is important to note that these daughters-in-law must have been of great character and quality for Naomi to have given out such emotional as well as prayer-laden words in *vs. 8-9*. Naomi wished them the three most important things a marriage can offer:

- A husband—spouse and companion
- A house—home which entails much more than the building; a house will require joy, happiness and love to be called a home
- Rest—this brings utmost glory and fulfilment out of all marriages; a home must have rest for God's glory to be evident in it.

Hard it is to part! The atmosphere became emotionally charged as she kissed them and as they wept together. The ladies wept for their dead spouses and thwarted love affairs; while Naomi wept for her husband and her sons, and perhaps for the childlessness of her daughters-in-law, as well as the loneliness that lie ahead for her.

> *And they said unto her, surely we will return with thee unto thy people. And Naomi said, Turn again, my daughters: why will ye go with me? Are there yet any more sons in my womb, that they may be your husbands?* (vs. 10-11 KJV)

After Naomi's first charge to them to go back, they insisted on following her to her people. Their loyalties to their husbands had ended, but they were still loyal to Naomi, even in the face of hopelessness. She made them understand how following her would be sheer foolishness. Naomi had resolved to accept her fate but wanted the best for her daughters-in-law who still had a chance to start life over.

> *Turn again my daughters; go your way; for I am too old to have an husband. If I should have a husband also tonight, and should also bear sons; would ye tarry for them till they were grown? Would ye stay from having husbands? Nay, my daughters, for it grieveth me much for your sakes that the hand of the LORD is gone out against me. (vs. 12-13)*

Typical of mothers, the predicament of Orpah and Ruth and their survival became Naomi's priority. Naomi knew that keeping them as relations was not possible any more. Her husband had died, hence, she could not get pregnant again even if she was still fertile. Even if she had a husband to impregnate her to give birth to sons—if it were possible—it would still be foolish of these ladies to wait for the boys to grow. Making them understand these intricacies, she implored them to *turn again* (twice more).

> *And they lifted up their voice, and wept again: and Orpah kissed her mother-in-law; but Ruth clave unto her. And she said, behold, thy sister in law is gone back unto her people, and unto her gods: return thou after thy sister in law. (vs. 14 – 15)*

The emotional atmosphere became so charged that they *"...wept again"*. Orpah must have counted the cost so well and examined Naomi's counsel. It is not stated anywhere in the Bible that Orpah did something wrong in departing from her sister-in-law, neither do I intend to offer any wrong view of Orpah. However, Orpah's position will be a lesson for us to learn from as we examine Ruth's decision and desire.

> *And Ruth said, entreat me not to leave thee, or to return from following after thee: for whither thou goest, I will go; and where thou lodgest, I will lodge; thy people shall be my people, and thy God my God: where thou diest, I will die, and there will I be buried: the LORD do so to me, and more also, if ought but death part thee and me. (vs. 16-17 KJV)*

Considering the words of Ruth above, we can extract these seven requests:

- That her plea be not hindered: entreat me not to leave you, or to return from following after you
- Where you go, I will go
- Where you lodge, I will lodge
- Your people shall be my people
- Your God shall be my God
- Where you die, I will die, and there will I be buried
- Jehovah do so to me, and more also, if anything but death should separate us

Only God can tell what was running in the mind of Naomi as Ruth gave these strong words of allegiance while sealing them with God's name. Whatever Ruth saw ahead in this encounter that gave birth to these words is not recorded in the Bible. In fact, the disposition of Naomi to her daughters-in-law was not stressed.

But since the usual marriage vow ends with *'til death do us part*, Oprah can be appreciated for following Naomi until after the third plea for them to go back. Her marriage with Chilion ended when Chilion died. She, as such, deserves our respect for being loyal to Naomi until this point.

However, Ruth's understanding of her marriage vows to Mahlon was unprecedented. *'Til death do us part,* to Ruth, meant something more, in that the *us* was not just her and Mahlon, but her and the entire lineage of Mahlon. It would take Mahlon's entire lineage being cut off before Ruth would turn back from the marriage. We can prove this from her seven pleas to Naomi. While many couples nowadays do not stand to fulfill the vow *'til death do us part* between each other, the death of Mahlon only called for a renewal of the vow in Ruth's case. Orpah must have considered salvaging her future and the rest of her life, while Ruth clave to a seemingly hopeless future.

Orpah returned unto her people while Ruth said *goodbye* to her past, never to return again come what may. She had bid her people goodbye, and neither Mahlon's death nor the turmoil that beclouded the rest of her life would make her renege. Whereas Peter (the Rock) returned to fishing after Jesus' crucifixion, Ruth displayed an allegiance not recorded anywhere else in the whole Bible.

Orpah returned unto her gods, but Ruth bade those gods a *goodbye*. Perhaps she had seen the God of Mahon. Thus, regardless of what hardship she was going to face, Ruth maintained the *goodbye* she had bid the gods of her land, declaring *your God will be my God.*

Reading through the Bible, no other human relationship has produced the allegiance Ruth had for Naomi. If we can imagine a few, they were not in the face of such hopelessness and despair. I tried spending some moments to consider what Naomi must have been thinking, and the only thing I came up with was her resolution not to bother Ruth any longer.

> *When she saw that she was steadfastly minded to go with her, then she left speaking unto her. So they two went until they came to Bethlehem... (vs. 18-19a KJV)*

The words of Ruth in *vs. 17* must have made Naomi to stop pressing for Ruth's going back. I imagine that Naomi had no option seeing that Ruth was resolute. Ruth's life just became the definition of perseverance.

Abraham, Manoah, Noah, Zachariah, Jeremiah, Moses, Elijah, Isaiah, Ezekiel and many others, related with God with all their strength and were loyal. However, Ruth did more. This woman dared odds, impossibilities and despair to become the grandmother of the famous King David and also one of the mothers in Jesus' lineage. I can remember that I once mentioned Ruth in one of the editions of *Selah Series* as the best wife a man can be privileged to have. The loyalty, commitment and everything she displayed even after Mahlon's death were all unprecedented. Of all the women in Bible history, aside from Mary, who by divine favour and blessing, became the mother of my Saviour, Ruth deserves a greater ranking.

> *So Naomi returned, and Ruth the Moabitess, her daughter in law, with her, which returned out of the country of Moab: and they came to Bethlehem in the beginning of barley harvest. (vs. 22 KJV)*

The Targum says that an angel had told Naomi of the new situation—famine being replaced with plenty—in Bethlehem and this turned out to be true. Elimelech had left his land for Moab because of famine. Whether he took the decision against God's instruction was not clearly stated in the scripture but it is significant to note that the trouble we mentioned in the first few verses of this chapter included the death of Elimelech and his two sons shortly before plenty returned to their native land, Bethlehem. Even though the entire scenario was hopeless, Naomi and Ruth were still able to rebuild their shattered hope.

Although the most evident virtue of Ruth is perseverance, I came across a few other virtues about her while exploring *Chapters 2-4*.

And Ruth the Moabitess said unto Naomi let me now go to the field, and glean ears of corn after him in whose sight I shall find grace. And she said unto her, go, my daughter... And she said I pray you let me glean and gather after the reapers among the sheaves: so she came, and hath continued even from the morning until now, that she tarried a little in the house. (Ruth 2 vs. 2, 7)

Her decision-making instinct, drive and intuition were as virtuous as her perseverance. *Go my daughter* was the response from Naomi. What I value in *vs. 2* is that Ruth had no need to be told what she was supposed to do. She knew their needs and she rose up to meet them. While another person in her position would have complained and groaned bitterly for days, Ruth decided to leave her hopelessness behind and to face the future.

Aside from Ruth's determination and diligence, her manners caught my attention too. Having ideas in some cases is not as important as being able to convince and get the support of others. In *vs. 2*, we saw how she was able to convince Naomi; and in *vs. 7*, we again saw how she was able to present herself and her ideas to the overseer of the labourers in Boaz's farm. Apart from possessing ideas, she made sure she initiated the actions needed to birth the idea. It is notable to state that many people have ideas but only very few take steps towards realising the ideas.

... and hath continued even from the morning until now is another clause that speaks much about Ruth's diligence.

The four chapters of Ruth, with 85 verses, are very interesting to study. They reveal the customs in Israel at the time, the relationship between Naomi and Ruth, and between Ruth and Boaz. It is edifying to identify a number of things that made Ruth a virtuous woman. Below are some of the her qualities, she is:

- Committed
- Morally upright
- Loving
- Humble
- Emotionally strong
- Respectful
- Approachable
- Presentable
- Discreet
- Intuitive
- Prompt
- Thankful
- Obedient to instructions
- Caring
- Kind to the latter
- Cultured
- Better than seven sons 4 vs. 15
- Patient
- Persevering
- Virtuous
- Diligent

Perhaps, there is no other qualification that a woman needs to be David's great-grandmother than all these! In her own case, perseverance meant standing firm to your course even when success becomes more impossible and going forward with purpose even when the destination becomes uncertain. Her time of life came but after days of turmoil, despair and hopelessness had all been experienced.

Perseverance in the Archives

But what if I fail of my purpose here? It is but to keep the nerves at strain, to dry one's eyes and laugh at a fall, and baffled, get up and begin again.

Robert Browning (1812-1889)

By persistence, drops of water hollow out a stone, a ring is worn away by use.

Ovid, Roman poet (43 BC – 17 AD)

For water continually dropping will wear hard rock's hollow.

Plutarch (Greek biographer)

Keep right to the end of the road.

Harry Lander (1870-1950), Scottish singer & a comedian

I am a kind of burr; I shall stick.

William Shakespeare (1564 – 1616), English Poet & Playwright

The drop of rain maketh a hole in the stone, not by violence but by oft falling.

Hugh Latimer (1485 – 1555), English Clergyman a Reformer

Yet he was confident that Great Britain would pull through, provided we persevere and we fight with the greatest vigor and tenacity...

Winston Churchill (1942, in a letter to the British Parliamentary during World War II)

Meany, however, determined to persevere and doggedly pushed his position successfully in both forums.

George Meany, an American shaper of politics during 1974's labour division in the US.

Like Coppola, he is considered among the most important and individualistic of contemporary directorial talents and can be counted upon to persevere despite few reverses.

Robert Altman made history in US movie despite his health challenges and all hardships.

Bishop Crumbley, in his letter, wrote of the growing understanding of our common faith but noted the need to persevere in the difficult task of expressing our unity.

Bishop Crumbley wrote in a letter to John Paul II of the Vatican Church in 1985.

37-year-old Steve Jones came back from an off-road motorcycle accident that kept him out of competitive golf for three years and became the unlikely US open champion... He credited the biography of golf legend Ben Hogan for inspiring him to persevere.

Former US Golf Champion in 1996

To avoid these evils, we must know how to distinguish between things to be avoided and those to be sought;

we must hate evil once it is recognized and love the good; finally, we must persevere in our undertakings for good and virtuous causes.

Erastus Desiderius wrote in the 16th century on intellectual and ecclesiastical history.

I do not merely urge you to persevere in this; I actually implore you to.

Lucius Annacus Seneca, Roman Philosopher & dramatist

In the name of the Irish people, we humbly commit our destiny to Almighty God who gave our fathers the courage and determination to persevere....

Irish declaration of Independence in 1919

If we persevere in the career in which we have advanced so far and in the path already traced, we cannot fail.

President James Monroe's first inaugural address on March 4, 1817

....and he therefore invites all the non-slaveholding states to band together, organize as one body, and make war upon slavery in Kentucky, upon slavery in Virginia, upon the Carolinas, upon slavery in all of the slaveholding states in the union, and to persevere in that war until it shall be exterminated.

Abraham Lincoln's words in 1858 on Divided House (Slavery)

Throughout the long and difficult period of Watergate, I have felt it was my duty to persevere, to make every possible effort to complete the term of office to which you elected me....

President Nixon while resigning on August 8, 1974

> The giant lives in this country, and you are the person appointed to punish him for all his wickedness. You will have dangers and difficulties to encounter, but you must persevere....
>
> *Extract from Jack and Beanstalk*

With heart fortified with these animating reflections, we solemnly, before God and the world, declare, that exerting the utmost of those powers, which our beneficent Creator had graciously bestowed upon us, the arms we have been compelled by our enemies to assume, we will, in defiance of every hazard, with unabating firmness and perseverance, employ for the preservation of our liberties; being with one mind resolved to die freemen rather than to live slaves.

Words of President Thomas Jefferson in 1775 as recorded by John Dickinson

Mrs. Cooke, after almost fifteen years of striving in the national championship, was finally rewarded for her perseverance.

US Tennis 1941 Champion being congratulated for her eventual victory after several defeats.

Miss Shirley Fry, a contender for the women's championship for sixteen years, was finally rewarded with success in winning her first American title at Forest Hills, just as she had been rewarded for her long perseverance at Wimbledon.

Ms. Fry, the winner of the 1956 Wimbledon woman's tennis singles

Perseverance finally paid off for Vinny Giles, who won the US Amateur championship after three straight years of finishing second.

Vinny Giles after winning Amateur golf championship in 1972

Lemieux also won the Bill Masterton Trophy for dedication and perseverance.

Lemieux, in 1993, won tne Bill Masterton Trophy along with Hart Memorial Trophy's most valuable player in the national hockey league.

Anthony's own achievement lay in her inspiration and perseverance ... and on July 2, 1972, the US Mint honoured her work by issuing the Susan B. Anthony dollar coin.

Women's right activist who in 1872 fought on women's right to vote in the US. Her 50 years' hurdle was posthumously granted in 1920. She had died in 1906.

Like other efforts in cloning, however, this work demanded perseverance – it took 277 tries at somatic cell nuclear transfer to create Dolly.

The first successful cloning (of a sheep) work was after 277 attempts.

The story of his struggle to obtain an education and to win his freedom illustrates his remarkable personal strength and perseverance.

Said of Frederick Douglass, African American anti-slavery leader in 1852.

White signifies purity and innocence; Red-hardiness, and valor; and Blue, vigilance, perseverance and Justice.

Interpretation of the US flag's colours

I was ready to work at night as well as day, and by the most untiring perseverance and industry, I made enough money to meet my expenses and lay up a little money every week.

Frederick Douglass in 1845 revealed how he escaped slavery.

Moissan's research on the compounds of fluorine and his success in isolating the element was remarkable not only for its applications to the chemical industry but for his ingenuity and perseverance in the face of failure by other chemists and hazards of working with the chemical.

French chemist Henri Moissan (1852-1907) discovered fluorine in 1886. He began his formal education late in the 1850s; became Professor of Toxicology in 1889 and Professor of inorganic chemistry in 1889; and won Nobel Prize for Chemistry in 1906.

You see, fellow-soldiers, that perseverance is more prevailing than violence, and that many things which cannot be overcome when they are together, yield themselves up when taken little by little.

Plutarch, the Greek biographer, wrote of Roman General Sartorius (1st Century AD).

His chief characteristic was a high and noble sense of duty. Munificent in disposition, untiring in industry, indomitable in perseverance, he lived a long, full life.

Culled from the biography of Bishop Robert Machray, the British clergyman.

Henry IV's genial informality, bravery, gallantry, perseverance in adversity, and readiness.... have earned him a special place in French history.

Said of King Henry IV of France (1553-1610) who restored stability after religious wars.

Sacagawea, carrying her young son on her back throughout the journey, was noted for her perseverance and resourcefulness.

The US Mint issued the new golden dollar coin in early 2000 to honour her efforts on US explorers, Jean and Clark between 1804 and 1806.

Part II

The Time of Life

The time of life is not the time of struggling, of hustling or of coping. It is rather the time **of life**. When the time of life comes for a poor man, he does not just get rich, he becomes wealthy. When it comes for a barren woman, she does not just bear children, she becomes blessed among mothers. Having considered the experiences of father Abraham, Ruth, the Israelites at the Red Sea and of course, the death of Lazarus, it is not outrageous to say that hard times, on most occasions, exist before the times of life.

The birth of Life Himself, in the form of a human being, was preceded by a precarious time between Mary and Joseph, which, if it were nowadays, would have resulted in a divorce. Hardly will a man of this age believe that his wife got impregnated by the Spirit and agree to keep same a secret. Worse still, living for months without sex with one's newly wedded wife, due to pregnancy and child birth, would have made things worse. In Part II we shall study other hard times as we draw insights from the word of God.

Part II will shed light on the happiness that floods one's heart or home when the time of life arrives; the fulfillment that follows the times of refreshing; and God's ability to work out the seemingly impossible.

Chapter 5

Is Anything Too Hard for the Lord?

In Part I, we discussed the hardship that Abraham and Sarah went through in spite of their obedience to God's words and statutes. They both ensured that their relationship with God was not affected in any way. This relationship brought about a repeat of Eden's experience in which God visited humans physically. *Gen. 18 vs. 1-33* reveals how the LORD, along with two other angels, visited Abraham in the tent, spent a good amount of time in his abode as they waited to dine and afterwards confided in him what was set to happen in Sodom.

And the LORD said, "shall I hide from Abraham that thing which I do..."? is one of the statements in the Bible that amaze me the most. He did not only grow to the level of hosting God and His entourage, he also became God's confidant.

It must be said, however, that beyond sacrificially obeying God's words, Abraham was also hospitable. He could have lost everything if he had not received the visitors as hospitably as he did. He welcomed God, entertained Him and offered the best he could, despite not having knowledge of who his guests were. *Gen 18 vs. 2* refers to them as *three men* and in *vs. 3*, Abraham said *My Lord*. How he recognised them as not mere humans is not stated in the Bible, but this indicate to us how Abraham had grown in intimacy with God despite his challenges. Better than Adam's privilege in Eden, God dined in Abraham's abode in Mamre and confirmed His first human confidant.

> *.... and they did eat. vs. 8*
>
> *And he said, I will certainly return unto thee according to the time of life; and, lo, Sarah thy wife shall have a son. And Sarah heard it in the tent door, which was behind him. Now Abraham and Sarah were old and well stricken in age, and it ceased to be with Sarah after the manner of women. Therefore Sarah laughed within herself, saying, after I am waxed old shall I have pleasure, my lord being old also? And the Lord said to Abraham, wherefore did Sarah laugh, saying, shall I of a surety bear a child, which am old? Is anything too hard for the Lord? At the time appointed I will return unto thee, according to the time of life, and Sarah shall have a son. Then Sarah denied, saying I laughed not; for she was afraid. And he said, nay; but thou didst laugh. (Gen. 18 vs. 10-15 KJV)*

Is Anything Too Hard for the Lord?

After blessing Abraham with the honour of eating in his abode, God resumed His primary aim of visiting by declaring Isaac's birth. I took note of a few phrases in the passage above.

...and he said

There is no record of failure against God. Before and after this passage, there has not been a case of Him failing to do what He had promised to do. So, the promise here is not coming from a fallible deity, but from the omniscient, omnipotent God. In fact, it came from God's mouth directly to the recipient of the covenant. He neither sent His angels as He did in Manoah, Elizabeth or Mary's cases, nor sent His Prophet. The declaration came from Him that *speaketh and bringeth to pass*. The person that *said* is the God that exalts His words above His name. The Word that had been in existence from the beginning with God and who Himself is God was the Prophet speaking here.

.... I will certainly return unto thee....

The One speaking needed not put *certainly* for Him to be believed, but then He puts it to affirm His words. This is why I marvel every time I read Jesus using words such as *verily, truly,* and *assuredly.* Even though His return might not be in the physical form anymore—of course He did not—He gave Abraham His promise of returning unto him. The *return* promised was the birth of Isaac and the *certainly* was fulfilled. In this visit, He ate; on His return, He fulfilled His promise, which Abraham had longed for.

... according to the time of life ...

This clearly confirms that there are processes and phases in the arrival of the time of life. In English usage, *according to* means *as stated or as reported by somebody or something; relying on somebody or something's authority; as stated or indicated by somebody; in the way that a plan or system stipulates; as determined by*, and so on. But I prefer to use: *in the way that a plan or system stipulates.*

God, therefore, must have planned that Abraham and Sarah would have their *time of life*, however bitter or hard, before His return—Isaac's birth. There is a time of life and that means not all the times contain life. If God had said *at the time of life*, it only means that there is a *time of no life*. Life, in essence, is not just breathing but a period of supply, answers, and happiness. *At the time of life* can then be interpreted as *the time of answers and supplies* to their desires while *time of no life* would mean those years of Sarah's barrenness.

Moreover, it is important to note that the time of life varies with different issues and requests. Of course, it was not *time of no life* concerning Abraham's relationship with God. It is great to know that stipulated times and seasons of life are only known to God.

God made me understand that all things He plans do at *the time of life* will be done, and that at *the time of life*, there will not be impossibility.

...Sarah thy wife shall have a son.

The time of life was what God was trying to let Abraham understand, that Sarah would have a son. This declaration was followed by mixed reactions. I appreciate the author of Genesis for inserting a notable clause as given in *18 vs. 11* that Abraham and Sarah were old and well-stricken in age and that it had ceased to be with Sarah according to the manner of women. Precisely, Abraham was 99 years old while Sarah was 89 years old. Her menstrual cycle, which is a necessity for feminine fertility, had been replaced by menopause. But God demonstrated here that it was not a *menostop* but only a *menopause*. He that paused what was necessary for fertility again *unpaused* it, and made the barren womb fertile in an age before the intervention of in vitro fertilization by the gynecologist or obstetrician.

So I did not find it hard to understand Sarah's position and thoughts. Rather, I found God so amazing to comprehend. To show His all-knowing character, He made it known that knew what Sarah was thinking and He confronted her with those words. He re-affirmed the declaration that He shall return unto them according to the time of life and that Sarah shall have a son. The question that starts *vs. 14* is what I prefer to end this paragraph with: **Is there anything too hard for the LORD?** The passage does not offer a direct answer to that question but I do: NO, NOTHING is hard for the LORD, not to mention too hard. For your own case, if He *unpaused* menopause for the 90-year old Sarah to deliver Isaac, then He can do much more to prove His worth in your case. Only believe Him and pray for your own season of life to come. If the time tarries, wait obediently for it. It will come and you will ask others the question—as you present your testimony—"Is there anything too hard for the LORD?"

The *Time of Life* for Rebecca and Rachel

> *And they sent away Rebekah their sister, and her nurse, and Abraham's servant, and his men. And they blessed Rebekah, and said unto her, Thou art our sister, be thou the mother of thousands of millions, and let thy seed possess the gate of those which hate them. (Gen 24 vs. 59-60 KJV)*

What a great prayer! Laban and Bethuel did not know who Isaac was, even though they knew Abraham. In fact, it was *Abram* they knew, not the blessed *Abraham* with whom God had covenanted Himself. They did not know therefore of the Lord's covenant concerning Isaac whom their sister was going to marry. In blessing Rebecca, they did not struggle to declare her a mother. They prayed for her to become *mother of thousands of millions*. Wow! And concerning Rebecca's thousands of millions children, they declared that—the unborn generations—to possess the gates of those that hate them. In other words, they declared fruitful a land that had not been cultivated, and they declared victorious an army that had not been born. This, of course, was a good send off for Rebecca and a good platform to build her marriage.

> *And Isaac intreated the LORD for his wife, because she was barren; and the LORD was intreated of him, and Rebekah his wife conceived. (Gen. 25 vs. 21)*

Knowing that Terah—his father—had to wait for years before he gave birth to his first child—Haran—and the many years of waiting for the promised "child"—child not children— then I feared greatly how the latter years of Abraham must have looked like. He had Isaac when he was 100, and Isaac married Rebecca when he was 40—Abraham at 140. He had to wait another 20 years before Rebecca became pregnant. If the covenant had stated "children of promise", then Abraham could have thought others would keep the promise alive. But Isaac's wife was also barren, which suggests the end of the promise.

To make worsen matters, Ishmael fathered many children. However, as fruitful as he was, the Bible depicted him as limited: his generation can be numbered. The reason is not far to seek: Isaac is the "child" of promise. So, in *Gen. 25 vs. 12*, the Bible listed the generations of Ishmael, while that of Isaac—who had the covenant—could not be numbered.

The woman whose people had declared to be a mother of thousands of millions was paradoxically barren, and had to wait for 20 full years. Although the Bible does not offer details of Isaac's behaviour and character during the 20 years of waiting, his prayer to the Lord, as seen in the passage above, suggests his reaction. *Entreat* in literal English means *to ask somebody to do something in a serious and often emotional way*. Perhaps for the 20 years, Isaac and Rebecca were busy entreating God. The role Abraham played in this process was not stated but we can reason that he prayed to God too, and most likely did his best to reassure and counsel his son, Isaac. Isaac gave birth to Esau and Jacob when he was 60 (Abraham was 160). This means that Abraham saw his "grandchildren of promise" and lived another (his last) 15 years with them.

Perhaps you will agree with me that a child of such promise, as given in *Gen. 17*, should not be childless in his lifetime. Alas, Isaac was! This tells us that He that promised us will definitely live up to His words and fulfill His promises, our hard times notwithstanding. Thinking that God's promises will be fulfilled without challenges, would be an error of judgement concerning the Lord God and His ways of fulfilling His promises.

> *And when the LORD saw that Leah was hated, he opened her womb, but Rachel was barren (Gen 29 vs. 31 KJV).*

The hatred towards Leah is more than the literal meaning of the word. It is an idiom, which means preference. Her sister, Rachel, was preferred by Israel. Three significant things are evident when we review *Gen. 29 vs. 15-35*:

- **Barrenness running in four successive generations:** We had established earlier that the wives of Terah, Abraham, Isaac and Jacob all experienced long delays in conception and childbirth. Considering the relationship between God and Abraham, together with the "everlasting covenant" in place (*Gen. 17 vs. 7, 13, 19*), one would have humanly concluded that no ill luck or misfortune could be experienced by these men. However, their infertility does not take away the truth that God loved them; that God had covenants with them; that God is omnipotent; and that God knew about their predicaments.

- **Crisis in a nuclear family running in three successive generations:** Sarah, having lost hope concerning her fertility, urged Abraham to sleep with Hagar. It was the same Sarah that picked the first stone and declared a war. This almost tore the family apart before Abraham stood up to settle the issues. Ishmael and Hagar had to suffer the consequences by departing their supposed house in order to make room for the manifestation of the child of promise (*Gen. 21 vs. 9-14*). Esau and Jacob had begun their rivalry while in their mother's womb. They continued this into adulthood. *Gen. 25 vs. 23-34; 27* offers the details of how Isaac's nuclear family rarely knew peace existing among them—for Isaac loved Esau while Rebecca loved Jacob. Again, under Jacob's roof, we see Leah and Rachel set against each other, despite being siblings of the same father (Laban).

- **The generals lied:** Reviewing *Gen. 12 vs. 12-17; 20 vs. 1-9; 26 vs. 6-11* and *27 vs. 14-29* reveals that God's generals were untruthful at different times for different reasons. Abimelech's experience caught my attention as he was deceived by Abraham and Isaac at different times and in the same place and for the same reason. His upright heart and God's intervention saved things. But Rebecca's plot concerning Jacob and Esau generated a totally different outcome. I thought that a man of Abraham's status, a child of covenant like Isaac and a preferred one like Jacob should be the last names on the list of people who at one time or the other lied to save their necks. I was wrong to think so. They lied on major occasions. My aim is not to castigate these great generals as liars, but to show that God, in His passionate love for them, pardoned and favoured them, their transgressions notwithstanding. When there is a relationship, His covenant becomes automatic; and wherever His covenant is, forgiveness and pardon dwell. An attempt to seek the latter will end in failure, if the former is not in place.

- **The request of Rachel that Jacob should sleep with her maid and bear children in her stead:** Sarah did this and the result was Hagar's expulsion from Abraham's house. So Bilhah became the mother of Dan and Naphtali (5th and 6th sons of Jacob, respectively).

And God remembered Rachel, and God hearkened to her, and opened her womb. And she conceived, and bares a son; and said God hath taken away my reproach: And she called his name Joseph; and said, The LORD shall add to me another son. (Gen. 30 vs. 22-24 KJV)

To remember implies that one had either forgotten—an unintentional act—or taken away one's mind from that which ought to be remembered—an intentional act. Since God cannot forget anything, being the all-knowing God, then, we can conclude that God had intentionally taken His countenance away from the plight of Rachel in those years. Hearkening to her became spontaneous after God remembered her. Opening her womb also affirms that He that shuts also has the power to open. He had initially shut her womb but what is important to us is not the word *shut* but *opened*. In essence, we can conclude that *the time of life* for Rachel had also followed a plan, a system "according to which" the birth of Joseph would come after years of barrenness. All efforts made in the *years of no life* would not produce any effect. However long the years after menopause, wombs shall again conceive and the barren shall be the mother of thousands of millions in *the time of life*.

It is astonishing to know that Rachel was the first woman in the Bible to prophesy and that her words were fulfilled long afterwards. I want to imagine Rachel as an optimistic woman who had been praying for years before Joseph's birth. She had been very emotional in accusing Jacob (*Gen 30 vs. 1-2*) to the point where Jacob became angry with her.

However, what is more important to our review is how she became so optimistic and used the privilege of Joseph's birth to request for yet another son. When your *time of life* comes, the years of barrenness, failures and reproach will be forgotten and replaced with seasons of gladness, happiness and answered prayers. But before the *time of life* it is a necessary to put in place a good relationship between you and the LIFE Himself. Regardless your past mistakes or failures, the chance to do exploits is still open and real if you do all to initiate and sustain your relationship with God.

Manoah's Time of Life

> *And there was a certain man of Zorah, of the family of the Danites, whose name was*

Is Anything Too Hard for the Lord?

> *Manoah; and his wife was barren and bare not. (Judg 13 vs. 2 KJV)*

While studying the scripture above, my attention was drawn to the first word in the verse: *And*. 'And' in the passage is a conjunction that joins Manoah's lineage to the situation within which Manoah's story becomes relevant. Thus, *vs. 1* got my attention.

> *And the children of Israel did evil again in the sight of the LORD; and the LORD delivered them into the hand of the Philistines forty years. (KJV)*

Reading through the book of Judges and other books of the Bible which begin with the word *And*, I discovered that *and* indicates the interrelatedness and connections among those verses and passages. However, in the verse above, *and* co-occurs with the word *again*, which then suggests that the children of Israel had done evil in God's sight in the past.

Manoah was the father of the 14th judge in Israel and the notable point to mark out here is that prior to his mention, and his own period as the judge in Israel, there had been issues between the Israelites and God which made Him deliver them into the hands of the Philistines. For the Israelites, when *the time of life* came—after the forty years, the Lord again sought for Himself a man that He would use to restore His people to Him.

But again, the chosen of the Lord was not forthcoming as expected. We do not know for how long they were barren, but the Bible says, "and his wife was barren, and bare not." This is neither like Sarah whose maid, Hagar, was made to bear Ishmael for Abraham, nor like Bilhah who bore for Jacob in Rachel's stead. Manoah's wife was barren and no maid bore any child for her husband in her place.

> *And the angel of the LORD appeared unto the woman, and said unto her, Behold now, thou art barren, and bearest not: but thou shall conceive, and bear a son. Now therefore beware, I pray thee, and drink not wine nor strong drink, and eat not any unclean thing; for, lo, thou shall conceive, and bear a son; and no razor shall come on his head: For the child shall be a Nazarite unto God from the womb; and he shall begin to deliver Israel out of the hand of the Philistines (Judges 13 vs. 3-5 KJV).*

The angel charged the woman and told her what was set to happen. As expected, the woman told her husband who did not doubt God's words but rather requested God to send the angel again to instruct them further on how to train the child. God answered the prayers of Manoah, and the angel was very patient with them during the next visit. He waited while Manoah's wife went to summon him, and waited also until a kid was prepared and the burnt offering was offered to the Lord.

I took note of a few things in the chapter. Aside from the fact that God was set to be reconciled to His people after forty years, I came to understand that Manoah must have been one of the few men left in Israel who had not gone with others to do evil in God's sight. To confirm this was Manoah's outright belief of what the angel said. We did not read it anywhere that Manoah or his wife doubted God.

Most times in the Bible, people tremble at the sight of God's angels, but not Manoah's wife (*vs. 2, 6*). Manoah was a man of prayers and faith in God (*vs. 8-9*). For the word *intreated to* have been used, it was not just a brief prayer, but serious, fervent and emotional supplications.

Manoah was also a hospitable and generous fellow (*vs. 15, 19*). Moreover, he was a man of gratitude (*vs. 17*), and he demonstrated all these to the angel who appeared the second time in human form (*vs. 20*), having appeared at first as an angel (*vs. 6*).

The point is that for God to deliver His people at this set time of life, He had to rely on His relationship with a man among His people. All the above points about the personality and character of Manoah would not have been relevant if he had not had a good relationship with God. He bowed at the awareness of the angel in a way that is heavily suggestive of his level of reverence for God. I must stress, however, that if God will set in to restore our land, our nation, and society to Himself, He will, no doubt, make use of the remnant among His people who had not bent their "backs" to "Baals".

Manoah was there when God needed a man in whose house the next judge shall be born, bred and nurtured for his mission.

I again found the instructions given to the mother on what not to do while the child was in her womb and when he would have been born very pertinent to our walk with God. This tells me that great men are not products of secular events and processes. They follow peculiar trends and consecrations. If a man must go all the way to fulfill destiny, he must identify the dos and donts of his destiny and comply with them as much as possible. As seen in the passage, Manoah's wife complied with the regimen as given by the angel. That Samson did not understand who a Nazarite unto God must be, especially in relating with women, was a failure that precluded a remedy. It is very important for you to discover the rules guiding your life and understand that breaching them means breaching your destiny.

> ...and he shall begin to deliver Israel out of the hand of the Philistines (vs. 56 KJV).

This caught my attention keenly. Out of the 17 Bible versions I studied, only two (TMB and BBE) have different words used in place of *begin*.

> *He will launch ... TMB*
>
> *He will take up ... BBE*

The remaining 15 versions used *begin*. I became surprised to see that Samson's destiny was not to come and conquer the Philistines completely and deliver his people; he was destined *to launch, to begin, to take up the process.*

David, at the point of defeating Goliath of Gath, almost looked like he was delivering the Israelites for forever, but the work of total deliverance was to be reserved for our Lord and Saviour, Jesus. Of course, the Israelites were no longer terrified by the Philistines after Samson's death; yet he only started the process of deliverance.

Finnis Dake stated that Samson and our Lord Jesus Christ were the only two men in Bible history who fulfilled the purposes of their destinies in their mortal deaths *(Judg. 16 vs. 30, Mt. 26 vs. 28, I Cor. 15 vs. 3, 2 Cor. 5 vs. 15, Gal. 1 vs. 4, Heb. 2 vs. 9-18).*

> *Manoah said unto his wife, We shall surely die, because we have seen God. But his wife said unto him, if the LORD were pleased to kill us, he would not have received a burnt offering and a meal offering at our hands, neither would he have shewed us all these things, nor would as at this time have told us such things as these (vs. 22-23. KJV).*

What a long but detailed response from a woman of sound understanding! The meaning of Manoah, *rest,* was set to manifest in his matrimonial life, even though the fear of seeing and conversing with God's angel almost turned his joy to grief. The response of Manoah's wife was profound. She gave a couple of reasons why God would not kill them and her words proved her knowledge of God. Why would God set out to punish, torment or disgrace you? He would not have led you this far only to embarrass you. He has good intentions concerning your tomorrow.

> *And the woman bare a son, and called his name Samson: and the child grew, and the LORD blessed him (vs. 24).*

The words of God through His angel became fulfilled without any delay. And the woman that *barest not* now gave birth to a son of purpose. The shame and reproach of barrenness was replaced with the joy of being the parents of the one God has anointed to initiate the deliverance of His people. When the time of life comes, all the shadows of sorrow and sadness will vanish, and become "Sun-like"—Samson—in God's glory.

Bitterness that Hastens the Time of Life:
Hannah's Time of Life in Shiloh

> *Now there was a certain man of Ramathaimzophim, of mount Ephraim, and his name was Elkanah, the son of Jeroham, the son of Elihu, the son of Tohu, the son of Zuph, an Ephrathite; And he had two wives; the name of the one was Hannah, and the name of the other Peninnah; and Peninnah had children, but Hannah had no children . . . . But unto*

Is Anything Too Hard for the Lord?

Hannah he gave a worthy portion; for he loved Hannah: but the LORD had shut up her womb (I Sam 1 vs. 1-2, 5 KJV).

Here again is a daughter of Abraham's lineage with the problem of barrenness. Elkanah was an Israelite, an Ephrathite, but his wife was barren. Ephraim, Jacob's grandchild, means *double fruit* and the land where they dwelled, Ephrath, means *fruitful*. Hannah married an Ephratithe and dwelled in Ephrath, but she was barren. What an irony!

I took a good look at *vs. 2*; the first of the two names were given as Hannah in their order of priority and coincidentally in alphabetical order, but when it came to their order of fruitfulness, Peninnah came first. I came to conclude that fruitlessness is relegated to take a second seat to other aspects of life. God is the Almighty that cannot be questioned and cannot be challenged.

Hannah means *gracious*, but why God decided to shut her womb is beyond human reasoning. Of all the women with a history of barrenness, we cannot lay claim to any of them being barren because of their sins—except for Michal. It seems more plausible that 'gracious' Hannah (who married a product of 'double fruitfulness' (Ephraim) and was residing in Ramat-haimzophim of 'fruitfulness'), should have been the mother of successive sextuplets; but God "had shut up her womb".

> *And her adversary also provoked her sore, for to make her fret, because the LORD had shut up her womb... Then said Elkanah her husband to her, Hannah, why weepest thou? And why eatest thou not? And why is thy heart grieved? Am not I better to thee than ten sons? (vs. 6, 7 KJV)*

Peninnah undoubtedly was an adversary because she provoked Hannah on a yearly basis since she had sons and daughters while Hannah had none. We can safely assume that there were many taunting remarks from Peninnah as she gloated over Hannah's childlessness. Even Elkanah, whose caring was worth more than ten sons, could not rescue Hannah from this home-bred mockery.

> *And she was in bitterness of soul, and prayed unto the LORD, and wept sore. And she vowed a vow, and said, O LORD of hosts, if thou wilt indeed look on the affliction of thine handmaid, and remember me, and not forget thine handmaid, but wilt give unto thine handmaid a man child, then I will give him unto the LORD all the days of his life, and there shall no razor come upon his head... (vs. 10-11 KJV).*

The passionate plea of Hannah above is one of the few detailed prayers in the Bible. Although there are different forms of prayer in the Bible, those like

Hannah's are not many. She had a cause, a reason and a purpose for praying. Her prayer was not routine or forced. She had a pressing need to pray and this prevented her from praying amiss as most believers do nowadays. She channelled her prayers rightly, from her heart to her God and with a sober mind and a passionate soul.

She also approached God on a solid ground—she was ready to give back to God that which she desperately wanted. Whereas, many in this age will prefer to visit church ministers and prophets, Hannah opted to commune directly with God and she left the temple with an assurance that God had heard her. She was persuaded that her prayer, during this trip to Shiloh, was different from previous ones.

I discovered that Peninnah was instrumental to Hannah's eventual happiness. The Holy Spirit made me understand that adversaries only help to strengthen the children of God in their endeavours. Hannah could have counted Elkanah as worth more than ten sons and refused to offer these words which called God to remembrance. Peninnah's taunts were aimed at distressing Hannah but they eventually provoked her to pray her way through.

Instead of getting down when your "adversaries" taunt or mock you, why not get provoked to pray to your God who sees and hears all things and answers your prayers? The persons whose lives we have reviewed so far in this part provoked and brought about their *times of life* by "entreating" God, by their earnest prayers and by remaining steadfast in the face of troubles. Complaints are not what will bring God's hands to action; your prayers will.

> *Wherefore it came to pass, when the time was come about after Hannah had conceived, that she bare a son and called his name Samuel, saying, Because I have asked him of the LORD.... Therefore also I have lent him to the LORD, as long as he liveth he shall be lent to the LORD. And he worshipped the LORD there. (vs. 20, 28 KJV).*

Like Abraham, Hannah did not see her prized asset, the answer to her prayer, as too valuable to be given to the LORD. As young as Samuel was (*vs. 24*), Hannah made up her mind to part with him by offering him to God. When sadness turns to joy, people often forget God. We tend to forget our vows and promises. But Hannah was not like that. In her praises and appreciation, she did not withhold Samuel from God. She gave the child to God in return. The 'LORD' was the recurrent name in *I Sam 2 vs. 2-10:*

> *And Elkanah went to Ramah to his house, and the child did minister unto the LORD before Eli the priest ... But Samuel ministered before the LORD, being a child, girded with a linen ephod. (2 vs. 11, 18 KJV)*

Is Anything Too Hard for the Lord?

Hannah must have been the happiest for becoming the mother of a priest! What a rare privilege! In *vs. 11* above, the "child" ministered unto the LORD before Eli. Even while he remained a child, he ministered "before" the LORD.

> *And the LORD visited Hannah, so that she conceived, and bare three sons and two daughters. And the child Samuel grew before the LORD. (2 vs. 21 KJV)*

The Lord, who shall not rob any man or woman of the portion he/she deserves, made it possible for Hannah, whose womb was shut, to conceive. Of course, the King who shut it down decided to "open it up" such that after Samuel, three other sons and two daughters were born to Hannah. The *time of life* comes with abundance. When Hannah requested "a man-child", she probably did not know that more children were coming.

John the Baptist: A Product of the Time of Life

> *There was in the days of Herod, the king of Judea, a certain priest named Zecharias, of the course of Abijah: and his wife was of the daughters of Aaron, and her name was Elisabeth. And they were both righteous before God, walking in all the commandments and ordinances of the Lord blameless. And they had no child, because that Elisabeth was barren, and*

> *they both were now well stricken in years.*
> (Lk 1 vs. 5-7 KJV)

Zacharias means *Jehovah remembers* while Elizabeth means *God is my oath*. In the passage above, three sentences caught my interest:

- They were both righteous before God;
- They were walking in ALL the commandments of God;
- They were blameless in God's commandments and ordinances.

Luke 1 vs. 5 provides a good introduction concerning this couple: Zacharias is introduced as a priest and his wife as a descendant of Aaron. *Verse 6* built further on that introduction by telling us how these people were blameless in the commandments and ordinances of God. They were righteous before God. It then becomes contradictory to discover in *vs.* 7 that the said righteous and blameless couple were barren, *"...and they both were now well stricken in years."* This suggests that they were unfortunate, and could no longer have a child due to their old age.

But why barrenness, of all things? Although the Holy Spirit had provided an answer, I must stress here that these couples were not barren as a result of their sins. They, in fact, had solid personal relationships with God. They were people of God's covenant. Having their names built around God, one would expect such a couple not to lack any good thing, at least not children. *Verse 7b* sounds as if childbearing was impossible. But Why? Possibly because those years might have brought them various successes in ministry and/or in other facets of life. But as far as childbearing was concerned, those years were *times of no life*.

> *But the angel said unto him, Fear not, Zacharias: for thy prayer is heard; and thy wife Elisabeth shall bear thee a son, and thou shalt call his name John. And thou shalt have joy and gladness and many shall rejoice at his birth. For he shall drink neither wine nor strong drink; and he shall be filled with the Holy Ghost, even from his mother's womb. And many of the children of Israel shall he turn to the Lord their God. And he shall go before him in the spirit and power of Elias, to turn the hearts of the fathers to the children, and the disobedient to the wisdom of the just; to make ready a people prepared for the Lord. And Zacharias said unto the angel, whereby shall I know this? For I am an old man and my wife well stricken in years (Lk 1 vs. 13-18 KJV).*

"... *and thou shalt have joy and gladness*" was the first thing that I took good note of in the above passage. It can be taken that God Himself knew they were not joyful in that aspect of their lives. Reviewing verses 7-

11 of the chapter, I came to understand that Zacharias was not praying for a child as at the time the angel appeared to him. He was just performing his tasks as the priest in the temple. *Thy prayer* must have meant *the prayers you have prayed before now.* He must have resolved in his heart to continue serving God in righteousness, blameless compliance— the barrenness of his wife, notwithstanding.

John—*Jehovah shows favour*—eventually came to actualise the meanings of Elizabeth and Zacharias, but *according to the time of life. Luke 1 vs. 14-17* reveals that the name really fits the child to be born. In fact, his purpose, like other children born after a long waiting, made the waiting worth it.

Reviewing *Gen 18 vs. 10-15* reveals Sarah's questions and thoughts about God's promise. In fact, she laughed at the promise. I compared Sarah's response with the question Zacharias asked Angel Gabriel. And worse still, when God confronted Abraham with Sarah's thoughts, the Bible says, *"Then Sarah denied..."* God did not punish Sarah for laughing at the prophecy, or for lying—by denying. But Zacharias was rendered dumb when he requested **a sign** from the angel. Perhaps God saw their hearts when they reacted to the good news. The angel affirmed that Zacharias doubted (*1 vs. 20*), and that was not recorded about Sarah.

> *And after those days his wife Elisabeth conceived, and hid herself five months, saying, thus hath the Lord dealt with me in*

> *the days wherein he looked on me, to take away my reproach among men... Now Elisabeth's full time came that she should be delivered; and she brought forth a son. And her neighbours and her cousins heard how the Lord had shewed great mercy upon her, and they rejoiced with her. (vs. 24-25, 57-58 KJV)*

Elizabeth hid her pregnancy during those initial five months in awe of what was happening. Being well-stricken in years, it must have been an extremely odd thing for the people around and neighbours to behold her carrying a pregnancy. Having not carried any pregnancy in her early years, the queerness of having to carry one became real. But what matters here is that the joy that the angel promised was already manifesting during pregnancy long before John was delivered (*vs. 25*). His arrival marked the beginning of the fulfilment of Angel Gabriel's words. The latter part of *vs. 58* reads, *"and they rejoiced with her."*

Whatever form of sorrow or reproach you might have carried for only God knows the number of years, people will still rejoice with you in Jesus name! Your cousins, relatives and neighbours will still gather to celebrate God's glory with you. Even if *well stricken in years* is applicable to your own case, you have to understand that *with God nothing shall be impossible (Lk 1 vs. 37)*.

That John's birth became possible signifies that your own much-awaited desires can still come to pass and that your "grace of Jehovah" will still come according to the *time of life*.

Rapid advancements in the world of science and technology are gradually shrinking our faith in God and what He can do. Our age is witnessing a time in which most spiritual and scriptural precepts are being tested against scientific discoveries, theories and speculation. Yes, we should celebrate all the advances in science (*Dan 1 vs. 4*), but we must know that "*...the letter killeth, but the spirit giveth life...*" (2 Cor. 3 vs. 6).

Hence, we must grow in knowledge of our world, but we must as well develop in the Spirit of God. We must not allow the advances in the knowledge of this world to quench our faith in Him. The purpose of this charge—this book—is to show us that these patriarchs did not turn their backs on God despite their challenges. In God's record, there is no late time, no delay and no disappointment. *He does all things to time. Your desires will come according to the time of life.*

Chapter 6

Beautiful Bethesda of Zarephath

And the word of the LORD came unto him, saying, Arise, get thee to Zarephath, which belongeth to Zidon, and dwell there: behold I have commanded a widow woman there to sustain thee. So he arose and went to Zarephath. And when he came to the gate of the city, behold the widow woman was there gathering of sticks: and he called to her, and said, fetch me, I pray thee, a little water in a vessel, that I may drink. And as she was going to fetch it, he called to her, and said, bring me, I pray thee, a morsel of bread in thine hand. (I Kg 17 vs. 8-11 KJV)

Prophet Elijah declared that a famine would occur in the land by the word of the Lord, that there would be no rain for three and a half years. And he had been fed in the early days of the famine twice daily by the angels of the Lord. Then God sent him to a widow and her son who were on the fringes of death. The first thing to note here is the word *widow*. We do not know how good her family story was while her husband was alive; we can only reason that things perhaps became worse for her and her son as the famine progressed. This woman got her positioning right—she was where her destiny had chosen for her to be in spite of her situation. Positioning in our own age has become another thing entirely as we all want to be in 'great' places not minding whether our own destiny lies there or not.

An hour discussion I had with my mentor in October 2005 helped me to make a good decision in the autumn of 2006. Professor Adesegun Fatusi had, in 2005, charged me that if I learn the "principle of positioning", things would be well with me. A year later, when my colleagues were flooding Lagos for the so-called better jobs, I remained in Ilesha. Eventually, I became God's agent through whom my colleagues got employed. Those two years I spent in the Castle of Mercy now rank as high as my baccalaureate experience in Obafemi Awolowo University. This widow was rightly positioned. Perhaps one would say God had ordered her to be there for the purpose of meeting the prophet.

How lovely it is to discover the word "gathering"! Regardless of what she intended doing with the sticks she was gathering, the word *gathering* means she was making her own efforts to make 'things' work for her. Many people are rightly positioned but remain idle. She was not the lazy type; she was busy doing something with her time. Taken that God has a great role to play in bringing your time of life, are you rightly positioned for your time of life? Are you doing something good at the moment?

The Lord told His prophet that the woman was a widow; her plight and challenges were not told to the prophet. So, Elijah did not hesitate to "pray thee" in demanding everything he wanted in order to make himself comfortable. "Sustain" was the word God used to describe how the woman will meet his needs. Thus, he must have had a good level of confidence in what the woman would offer. The first thing Elijah requested was for a drink in a vessel and next to that was a morsel of bread in her hand. God's word had sent Elijah there to have him sustained by this widow, and all his demands were what the widow could provide to sustain the prophet.

Her Outburst

> *And she said, As the LORD thy God liveth, I have not a cake, but an handful of meal in a barrel, and a little oil in a cruse: and behold I am gathering two sticks, that I may go in and dress it for me and my son, that we may eat it and die.*

Recognising that Elijah was a prophet of God, this widow did not hesitate to rise up and fetch Elijah water to drink. She had water and did not hoard what she had from the prophet's use. For some women, being ordered by a prophet would have made them either "request" for a miracle from God's prophet or shun him completely. But the widow did not opt for either of the two. This is unlike most believers today who, rather than give, will always demand as if that is why we were created. She did not shun him; she offered the prophet water in a vessel instead.

Before complaining about what she lacked, she was generous with the little she had. Reviewing her words in the verse above, she still had respect for God's prophet in spite of her anguish. She declared her assets and her plans. I want to imagine those times prior to Elijah's visit as *times of no life* for the widow. I imagine how uncomfortable she must have been in the process of opening up her mind to Elijah. We could assume that she would have offered the things Elijah requested if she had them.

Her Rare Hospitality and Reward

> *And Elijah said unto her, fear not; go and do as thou hast said; but make me thereof a little cake first, and bring it unto me, and after make for thee and for thy son. For thus saith the LORD God of Israel, the barrel of meal shall not waste, neither shall the cruse of oil fail, until the day that the LORD sendeth rain upon the earth. And she went and did according to the saying of Elijah: and she, and he, and her house, did eat many days. And the barrel of meal wasted not, neither did the cruse of oil fail, according to the word of the LORD, which he spake by Elijah. (vs. 13-16 KJV)*

Elijah, I am sure, was not selfish or greedy when he told the widow to first prepare cake for him. It must have been because of his understanding of God. God would not have sent him to a widow for him to be sustained without making provision for him in the woman's house. She did according to Elijah's words regardless of her difficult situation and Elijah's unusual command. Her obedience here is rare as she did not hesitate in executing Elijah's words. She did not rebuke Elijah for his request, rather she provided, with rare generosity, what the prophet requested.

If you want to be enriched, you must be ready to give away, as a sacrifice, that which you have in your hands. The *time of life* for this widow and her entire house required her right positioning, "gathering", prompt obedience and a high level of generosity.

What drew my attention to this passage was how God provided for His prophet to be sustained by a widow who only had a single meal, and had decided to die along with her son afterwards. What I found motivating was the generosity that this widow had to show for her *time of life* to break forth. The barrel and the cruse of oil did not go empty while famine ravaged the land. Irrespective of how poor or discouraging your own case might seem, making an uncommon sacrifice might usher in your *time of life*.

However unpleasant life seems to you, wear a good face, receive people with a fair heart and respect everyone around you. It is foolish to allow your condition to decide your mood and countenance. Let your mood be good; do not make a habit of complaining and learn to give more than you hope to receive. 'Whatever goes around comes around' is an ageless English adage and you will not regret being generous.

In some instances, people become wasteful in the name of being generous. I expect you to be discrete and to allow the Holy Spirit to guide you on when to be generous and when to conserve that which you have in your hands. The good news for you is that while you are busy preparing to quit hoping, and you think "death" is the next option you must take, He that decides the *time of life* might just have ordered His prophet to be sustained in your house. And His plans are great concerning you! What is next for you is to become a fountain where people around you will find solace for their souls and be sustained. See it!

38 Years Waiting for the Angel

One of my favourite Bible stories as a child was that of a lame man that had been at the pool at Bethesda for 38 years before the arrival of Jesus. This story is intrigued me, as it featured an angel who only comes once a year and to give out a competitive slot. As a child, I remember that I was able to convince people in the children church that only the deaf and/or dumb would have a good outcome on a yearly basis. My reasons are not difficult to understand—the blind and the lame would find it hard to compete for the slot because the competition would require eyes and legs.

Now there is at Jerusalem by the sheep market a pool, which is called in the Hebrew tongue Bethesda, having five porches. In these lay a great multitude of impotent folk, of blind, halt, withered, waiting for the moving of the water. For an angel went down at a certain season into the pool, and troubled the water: whosoever then first after the troubling of the water stepped in was made whole of whatsoever disease he had. And a certain man was there, which had an infirmity thirty and eight years. (John 5 vs. 2-5 KJV)

Here again is another detailed introduction in the Bible. The presence of the man at the poolside was first discussed before the duration for which he had waited was mentioned in the passage. It was amusing as a child to know that the angel came into the pool and "troubled" the water so that whosoever first stepped in would have his/her infirmities erased forever. The pool was close to a sheep market and more than that, the pool had five porches where competitors lay "waiting" for the angel.

Charles Darwin's theory of the survival of the fittest and the elimination of the weak must have worked greatly against this man. He would have been in the porch waiting for the angel. But it was not possible, that the person who would assist would not want to lose a annual chance by helping another candidate for the sole slot.

Bethesda means *house of mercy*, but this man had laid there for 38 years without encountering the needed mercy. We do not know what this man was doing in those hopeless years, but we can assume that, just like most crippled persons then who were situated close to the market, he would have, most likely, been a beggar. If begging was not his primary purpose there, it would have become a necessity to at least keep his body and spirit together.

Another important thing is that the longer he stayed, the more discouraged he got concerning a possible chance at healing. He had spent 38 years *of no life* at the supposed house of mercy without experiencing the mercy that he so much needed.

He Only Needs Your Answer, Not Explanation: "Wilt Thou Be Made Whole?"

> *When Jesus saw him lie, and knew that he had been now a long time in that case, he saith unto him, Wilt thou be made whole? The impotent man answered him, Sir I have no man, when the water is troubled, to put me into the pool: but while I am coming, another steppeth before me. (John 5 vs. 6 – 7 KJV)*

Jesus Christ was on his way to Jerusalem for a feast of the Jews and had to pass through this place. The One

Who decides the *time of life* passed through a supposed cemetery! It was very late before I learnt the questioning rule of Jesus. One of the Yoruba adages explains a case in which someone asks a question despite knowing the answer. I can recollect scenarios where, as a child, I got angry with people asking such a "needless" question.

But to Jesus, those questions are "needful". Surgeons, however obvious the need for surgery appears, will still require that the patient or a close relation fill and sign a consent form in the presence of a witness before they go ahead with the procedure. Informed consent is an ethico-legal issue which cannot be ignored in a medical environment.

Wiser than the wisest of surgeons, I see our Saviour complying with the ethico-legal, informed consent rule. According to *Mt 7 vs. 8*, *he that asketh receiveth*, not *he that wisheth* or *needth*. Hence, I got used to the principle of my Lord asking questions, however obvious the answer, just to ensure the person that needs His hands asks for them. He asked this man, but rather than answer with a straightforward "yes" or "no", the man went ahead only to explain. But that was not the answer to the question. "Yes" or "No" was. Eventually, my Lord got a "Yes" as the man explained how he had made an effort to step into the pool for healing.

Again, we see another person making a good effort even during *time of no life*. ...*but while I am coming* means that every time they knew the angel came, regardless of the large multitude *(vs. 3)* involved in the competition, this man still made his own attempt even in 38 failed episodes.

Sir is another word I found captivating as I sifted through the fine details from the passage. He, of course, did not know Jesus, but he had a sound character. The gestures and contents of your character will go a long way to decide how early or late your time of life comes.

Rise! It's Your Time of Life

> *Jesus saith unto him, Rise, take up thy bed and walk. And immediately the man was made whole, and took up his bed, and walked: and on the same day was the Sabbath. The Jews therefore said unto him that was cured, it is the Sabbath day: it is not lawful for thee to carry thy bed. He answered them, He that made me whole, the same said unto me, Take up thy bed, and walk (vs. 8-11 KJV).*

Had this man known who he was conversing with, he would have saved himself the stress of explaining. He did not know he was in front of the Word, the Way, the Truth, the LIFE, the Son of God. And upon the arrival of his *time of life*, the first word that proceeded from the mouth of Jesus was not "sorry" but *RISE*. The man was not up until the statement had been completed.

I want to imagine what must have been in his mind those milliseconds after the declaration. He could have seen *the man* as another mocker. But upon the completion of that declaration, he did not just rise, He rose prominently in the manifestation of God's glory. *And immediately the man was made whole*, for me, is a total healing of all the man's infirmities.

I have never, at any time, gone through *vs. 10-14* of the passage without taking some seconds to laugh at the response of the Jews towards the healing of this man. None of them congratulated him, not even for being liberated from a 38-year helplessness. They even told him that he should not have taken up his bed to walk. When your *time of life comes*, it is important for you to know that people around, whom you would expect to congratulate you, might gang up against your rising. They might go as far as challenging or questioning how you made it; they might give reasons you should remain a failure.

But rather than adopting a secular response such as arguing or picking a fight with them, why not adopt the protocol this man followed? Simply refer them to Him Who made you whole; to the Lord Who has exalted you and promoted you from stagnation to prominence. He did not know it was Jesus. He did not even ask Him for His name or address—like Manoah asked the angel. To him, he had seen an option better than the visiting angel's and had got what he wanted. When he was quizzed, his response was simple, clear and brief: "He that made me whole, the same said unto me…"

When It is your own *time of life*, rise up and be prominent. Adopt this wisdom to answer your critics by referring them to Him that made you prominent.

To Avoid Relapse, Sin No More

Certain medical ailments are curable if treatment process is duly followed. But if the process fails, the disease may relapse and relapsed ailments are worse and more difficult to manage than the initial ailment.

> *Afterward Jesus findeth him in the temple, and said unto him, Behold; thou art made whole, sin no more, lest a worse thing come unto thee. The man departed, and told the Jews that it was Jesus, which had made him whole. (vs. 14-15 KJV)*

It's a great opportunity for you to rise. You will become privileged and enabled to dine at great feasts with the prominent people of the land. This man made his way into the temple and had the privilege of seeing Jesus again. Just like most surgical or medical treatments come with precautions and advice to prevent relapse, the healing of this man also had a precaution: *sin no more*.

If God decides to lift your head, then avoid sin, otherwise, the pitfall would be worse than where you started. To remain up, *no sin* must be your dress code, pin code, password or watchword. The Jews had their reasons for attempting to attack Jesus, which is not your problem. He will deal with them according to His wisdom and power. Yours is *sin no more*. Had Jesus just given out the precaution alone without the possibility of a relapse, the advice would not have been complete. But Jesus gave him what the outcome of a relapse would be. He later went in his excitement to answer those asking him about "that man" who had healed him. It was Jesus! I do not know for how long you have been on this spot. *Rise*, take up thy bed, and walk.

"Immediately": the Language of *the Time of Life*

> *Now Peter and John went up together into the temple at the hour of prayer, being the ninth hour. And a certain man lame from his mother's womb was carried, whom they laid daily at the gate of the temple which is called Beautiful, to ask alms of them that entered into the temple. (Acts 3 vs. 1-2 KJV)*

Jesus had to leave before His disciples grew into the full stature of ministers. Their CVs did not have much content under "work experience" in spite of their lofty and admirable "educational training" for three and a half years with Jesus. What is significant in *vs.* 2 is that this man was born lame and had never walked in his entire life. He had been carried from one place to another since the beginning of his life and "laid" at the temple's entrance. Every time I enter a church, temple, chapel or any other worship centre and I see beggars with different infirmities at the entrance, certain thoughts and questions rush into my mind. Can't "these beggars" progress from the gate into the church, converse with God and have their healing? Are there children of God who enter and leave that church without any "that which I have I give unto thee?" Is God present in those worship centres?

Later I understood that God could dwell in those churches, but the beggars at the gate remained with their infirmities, because they did not believe. It is equally possible that the beggars believed but stood at the gate of a church without the presence of God. He is omnipresent; we can, for any reason, boast of the availability of our God. Thus, God's presence, when available, will work things out in the presence of faith and vice versa.

The nowadays disciples who go in and come out of the temple, without a declaration that can make a difference for beggars, adds to my submission that the congregation is growing while the church is shrinking. Is it because these believers lack the courage to act, that the "beautiful" temple's gate has become an office for beggars? The temple should be a place where people go to forget their problems. The lame man was carried and laid at the gate of temple every day. They carried him from home in the morning and laid him at the gate on a daily basis. He must have known many of the people worshipping in the temple. He must have known the various songs sung in the temple during worship. He would have heard different sermons at different times of his life at the beautiful gate. There is no mention of any attempt he made in the past to facilitate his healing. His only effort was begging and his profit was alms. Unlike the widow of Zarephath and that of the lame man at Bethesda, this man had accepted his fate, and had learned to live with his affliction.

What Are You Expecting?

> *Who seeing Peter and John about to go into the temple asked an alm and Peter, fastening his eyes upon him with John, Said, "Look on us", And he gave heed unto them, expecting to receive something of them. (vs. 3-5 KJV)*

Like every beggar, he would have been used to the fact that some people would just walk past him without even looking at him, not to talk of giving him anything. He would have as well known that some would give alms without his having to raise his voice before they do.

So when this man saw Peter and John, he begged for alms as the situation looked promising. *Begged* entails that he requested for the alms in a very humble way, perhaps with words of prayers, to force something tangible out of their pockets. I want to believe he had been glad to have Peter and John standing in front of him. He must have raised his voice and increased the words of his prayers in expectation of what these men would give him.

But a drama loomed when Peter could not bring out his wallet; rather he *fastens his eyes*. And to increase the tempo of the event, John looked the same way. Peter even requested that he look on them as if to mean 'we will give you your expected daily income now'. His expectations were not higher than alms. He probably did not expect anyone who knew his situation to 'park' in front of him and unleash any drama, however interesting. So he gave them his gaze, with the hope of receiving alms.

Better Than Your Request

> *Then Peter said, silver and gold have I none; but such as I have, give I thee: in the name of Jesus Christ of Nazareth rise up and walk. And he took him by the right hand, and lifted him up: and immediately his feet and ankle bones received strength. And he leaping up stood, and walked, and entered with them into the temple, walking, and leaping, and praising God... . And they knew that it was he which sat for alms at the Beautiful gate of the temple: and they were filled with wonder and amazement at that which had happened unto him. (vs. 6-8, 10 KJV)*

The man must have been worried seeing that these disciples did not dip their hands into their pockets. His disappointment must have increased when the disciples said they had no alms to offer him. 'What kind of guys are these, oh God'? the man must have asked himself. Other worshippers who were entering the temple while Peter and John engaged him may have looked promising to him in terms of alms. It must have been another crisis hearing Peter say, "rise up and walk". Rising must have been the language of another realm in his ears. He must have disliked them with a great passion as he wondered why on earth they decided to mock him seeing they had nothing to offer.

It is amazing to read how the man who was born lame rose, walked, jumped and praised God. But Peter had to go the extra mile. He probably understood that this man had not walked all his life and that he would not, if not aided. Peter then held his right hand and, more than that, he lifted him up.

At Bethesda, the command was all that was necessary to completely take care of 38 years of helplessness. But here, the command and a helping hand were required. The man did not make any effort on hearing Peter. The command was strange in his ears.

This event was a *time of life* in the ministry of Peter as well, as failing here could mar his courage on subsequent occasions. Peter had to do more of holding and lifting, not just commanding. You can equally do more.

Furthermore, it was the *time of life* for the man who had left his house to beg, only to behold himself upright, taller than he had ever been. At his *time of life*, the rigid ankle, knee, hip joints, idle muscles and all other structures in his lower limbs obeyed the command, as Peter and John held and lifted him. The body complied with the new-found lifestyle immediately. "Immediately" describes the pace of events that happens when the *time of life* appears and wipes away the sorrow of those years of hopelessness.

We can probably assume that the man had rarely entered the temple, if ever. All the same, like the man at Bethesda, who joined the Jewish feast, this man became fit enough to enter the temple and to participate in the 3p.m. worship. He did not postpone his privilege; he entered the temple with them, this time, not as a beggar. Some who had given him alms on the way to the temple now saw the same beggar happy as he had never had cause to be, jumping as he had never been able to do, and praising God as he had never had the opportunity to. Regardless your age or how long your *time or years of no life*, when your *time of life* comes, everything gains life immediately.

Chapter 7

Time of Refreshing

When the *time of life* comes, a person is refreshed. Time of refreshing comes with one's *time of life*. The dictionary meaning of the word *refreshing* is revealing. It is an adjective that means *pleasantly new or different, making you feel less tired or hot*. In the Encarta dictionary, it means *restoring energy, serving to restore energy and vitality, pleasing and rather exciting*, and *pleasingly different and exciting*.

The time of refreshing will then mean the time in one's life when one's energy is restored; when vitality replaces tiredness, and pleasant and exciting moments succeed all the sorrows and shadows of past pains, sins, losses and failures. The time of refreshing can then be expressed as a *time of life* characterised by renewal, vitality, vigour, strength, pleasantness and exciting experiences.

This chapter offers a new perspective on the *Time of Life*. We shall study Peter's statement in *Acts 3 vs. 19* as we trust the Holy Spirit to instruct us.

> *So then, let your hearts be changed and be turned to God, so that your sins may be*

completely taken away, and times of blessing may come from the Lord.

Repent therefore and be converted, for the blotting out of your sins, so that times of refreshing may come from (the) presence of the Lord. (DBY)

Repent therefore and turn again, that your sins may be blotted out, that times of refreshing may come from the presence of the Lord. (RSV)

Repent then! And reform, for the blotting out of your sins, so that there may come times of refreshing from the presence of the Lord. (MNT)

Repent, therefore, and reform your lives, so that the record of your sins may be cancelled, and that there may come seasons of revival from the Lord. (WNT)

Repent, then, and turn to God, so that he will forgive your sins. (NLT)

Now change your mind and attitude to God and turn to him so he can cleanse away your sins and send you wonderful times of refreshment from the presence of the lord. (TLB)

Now it's time to change your ways! Turn to face God so he can wipe away your sins, pour out showers of blessing to refresh you. (TMB)

So repent (change your mind and purpose); turn around and return (to God), that your sins may be erased (blotted out, wiped clean), that times of refreshing (of recovering from the effects of heat, of reviving with fresh air) may come from the presence of the Lord. (AMP)

Exploring different Bible versions of this verse helps us to have a good view to the much awaited *time of life*. We must understand at this point that the chain of the time of refreshing takes a course that must not be broken. And if followed to the letter, it guarantees the beginning of an individual's life in ease and vitality.

You Are the Decisive Factor

Over the past centuries, Christians have reasoned that God decides everything while others may argue that Fate is the cause behind everything. By so doing, we completely forget how our actions and decisions facilitate or hinder the intervention of God. We tend to believe that with or without our own efforts, God is still the one behind all things. Reviewing *Acts 3 vs. 19*, one fact rings through all the versions: YOU are the decisive factor. In fact, YOU, not God, decide the chain of events leading to your *time of life*.

Repent, reform and *change* were the words used by Bible writers to hang the entire responsibility of this decision on your shoulders. God is not going to reform or change you, or force you to repent: you will have to confront this significant task yourself. You will have to change your mind and attitude; you are the owner of the mind and creator of the attitude. For God to work on you, His creature, you will have to work on what you have created first. Although He has the power to do all things as He wills, the Bible makes us understand that He will not do some things. Salvation is free, but it will not be forced on anyone and it will not come like every other gift: YOU will kick-start the process by *repenting, reforming and changing* from your sinful ways.

The time of refreshing will only become a reality after your decision and action. Praying when you ought to act is a foolish mistake that will only land you in a hopeless and helpless destination. The most important thing now is not to *fast and pray* to God to bring that much awaited time of refreshing. *Repent, reform, and change!* If you do not do these, nothing can happen.

Turn (Back) Again

Be converted, turn and *reform* were the words used in the different versions of the Bible to describe the second stage on the chain. Having repented from your sinful ways, beliefs and attitudes, the next thing expected of you is to be converted. To be converted means that you will look away from sin and focus on God. It also means that you are ready to live a life that values and upholds righteousness. To be a convert means that you are resolute on *not going back*, in spite of the pressure to backslide *(1 Cor. 4 vs. 11-13, 11 Cor. 4 vs. 8-12)*

Turn again (RSV) shows that there had been a turning before. When He created you, He completed the job in such a way that guarantees and enables you to directly interact with Him. But that initial turning away from Him left you in the arms of the wicked one whose primary aim is to take you away from your Saviour.

Turn back (YLT), *Turn to God* (NLT) and *Turn to face God* (TMB) all buttress the fact that you are facing the wrong direction and that it is your repentance that will make you *turn to face him.* The sin, that He cannot behold, has made Him close His eyes from you while you turn your back at Him. He did not turn away! So, by coming to Him in repentance, you will cause His eyes to open to you again. It is now left for you to turn back again to face Him.

It must be added that this is a crucial stage that you cannot skip; He will rather give you space to go your way. He will open His eyes when you come to Him at the junction of repentance. But turning from sin to righteousness should be your only decision, aided by the conviction of the Holy Spirit.

One of the most significant eye-openers of the year (sometime back) was how God led me in a rare review of *Matthew 25 vs. 1-10*. At the end of those teaching sessions, I concluded that our hope at His coming will be glorious if the church would be as wise as the five foolish virgins.

These foolish virgins enrolled and waited for the Bridegroom. On the contrary, many in our auditoriums are not yet enrolled in the race to heaven. The congregations are getting larger, as Satan has successfully simplified our definition of being a Christian to mere church attendance.

To worsen the whole matter, the Biblical priests and prophets, who dared kings and who did not value their lives, are a rare breed in this new millennium. Atheists and priests in our age have many things in common and do things together. We are over stretching tolerance as light coexists with darkness without any issue. Motivational speakers sweep our altars most Sundays, and rather than preach salvation to the congregation, they "encourage" sinners to continue in their ways. Many servants of God lack the boldness to confront the sinfulness of their church members because their own lives are not exemplary. In short, many people in our congregations are not enrolled as the foolish virgins were.

The foolish virgins had their lamps. How unfortunate it is to know that many of us in the church today do not have lamps to light our path, although we are enrolled. This is the reason many stumble into difficulties and easily retreat to their old ways. The word of God is the true lamp to a Christian's feet, but when people are led to Christ with half-truth as "come to Jesus and you will know no pain again," then withdrawing is inevitable for such believers fed with such deceit.

It is significant that the foolish virgins had oil in their lamps. The Holy Spirit is the source of oil for a believer, but certain denominations cannot boast of the gift of Holy Spirit today. A common event between the wise and the foolish virgins was that they all slept off when the Bridegroom delayed in His coming. It is notable that the foolish virgins also heard the cry when the Bridegroom arrived. Many of us in this age are asleep and not even the noise of a train or the roar of a lion would awaken our souls from this self-induced coma. The foolish virgins heard the cry.

A critical issue here is that many Christians are holding lamps that have been out of oil for decades. It is either that some do not know, or those who know decide to forge ahead since they can still see with the lamps around. It is no controversy that many Christians cannot boast of a personal well-lighted lamp, and still, *it is well* is the slogan of everyone when almost everything is not well. Rather than deny the challenge like many of us would do, the foolish virgins confronted their own problem first by begging their counterparts for oil and later by daring the dangers of the dark to search for oil.

Our egocentric nature sometimes makes it hard for us to bend our backs and apologise when we are wrong. Many will also prefer to burn in hell than beg their way to heaven. The foolish virgins begged. We must note as well that they did not hold back their money for the oil. Money was not their problem: *time was.*

Being as wise as the "foolish virgins" in your own case would then mean enrolling now. If you have not hitherto, get the *lamp now* and fill it with *oil now*. You must assess your lamp *now* to discover if it is lighted or not; and if not, take the appropriate steps to get it lighted. Rather than beg agonizingly later, you can rush out now, that it is not yet dark to get the *oil* that can sustain you for the waiting period. No matter the stage you are, you still have the time now that the "Cry" of His coming is only being preached and not yet declared by angels.

Time was not in favour of the foolish virgins because they slept off as if they had oil. Had they not slept off, they would have discovered their need for oil and could have acted promptly. Do not sleep off; act now to save your destiny. This is another task that you must oversee in order for you to ensure your time of refreshing.

If You do

The verse in *NLT* ends with *If you do*. Please take a lot of time to ponder on: *if you do not do*. Before *if you do* in the verse, *he will forgive your sins* were the last words in *NLT* version of the verse. Another clause that must be stressed at this stage is the potency of your decision to repent, turn back and be wise, as well as the consequences of your refusal to act. Your much anticipated 'time of refreshing' is now a function of your decisions and actions.

Zaccheus, Peter, Paul and many other disciples did not find automatic jerseys on Christ's team; they took decisions and acted them out. Wait a bit! The beneficiaries of His signs and wonders did not get automatic attention; my Lord asked them. Even when He knew what they needed, He asked them if they wanted to be made whole. This is only to further stress that He who can decide your *time of life* will do so only if you are ready. If you do, He will forgive your sins. The challenge here is the clause: *if you do not do*. Definitely, it will not be wrong to say that He will not forgive you your sins if you do not repent, reform and change from your sinful ways. And if your sins are not forgiven, then the time of refreshing you anticipate will never come.

Can you imagine the strength of your position? If your time of refreshing does not come, those lives and destinies that your time of refreshing should positively affect may also lie fallow for long or even for their lifetime. So, the choice you make will not affect you alone, but also people around you. Your time of refreshing is then a product of *if you do*.

Your Sins Are Completely Blotted Out

If you repent, reform, change, turn back and take the wise steps now, then your sins will be completely blotted out. Your sins will be cancelled, wiped away, erased, and forgiven. By so doing, you will create a new platform on which you can start a life full of vitality, ease and grace.

The woman in the city, who was a sinner, (*Lk 7 vs. 37-50*) did not rob herself of the privilege of a time of peace. Although she did not outrightly follow the steps, she nonetheless washed the feet of Christ with tears and wiped them with the hair on her head. Afterwards, she broke her alabaster box of ointment to anoint Jesus' feet.

But why the tears? That must be a product of true repentance and sober reflection. She did not consider her glory, her hair, as too precious to serve as towel for her Lord. The tears, enough to wash, must have run like a fountain from the woman's eyes. She sacrificed her glory and her expensive ointment to anoint Christ's feet. She must have drawn the attention of people around her in the process but right there, she got her reward: *Thy sins are forgiven.*

All that the destiny of the woman needed was four words of 18 letters from Him who is able to forgive. *Thy sins are forgiven* was then followed by *Thy faith hath saved thee.* Faith can only be built on forgiveness of sins and the most important send-off words: *Go in peace.* Forgiveness is the ground on which faith is built and faith is the premise on which peace can thrive. The most important blessing a sinner can get from God is *Thy sins are forgiven*. If you are a sinner and you keep praying for a time of refreshing to come, you may spend a lifetime praying without any result until you follow the steps that can save your destiny from destruction. This woman did not get *go in peace* as an answer to prayers from Jesus. It came after her decision and actions. The *time of life* is a time of refreshing and peace but it comes after *Thy sins are forgiven*.

Most of the versions end the verse with *from the presence of the Lord*, and that is the utmost part of this review. Your repentance and your turning back are unto God. Your sins can only be forgiven by God. And the good part is that it is only from the presence of the same Lord that your anticipated time of refreshing can come. In His presence is the fullness of joy that your soul craves. But you cannot dwell in His presence with your sins.

After fulfilling your own part of the process, the supply and upkeep of your life of refreshing become God's responsibility. But like a surgeon who must not perform surgery on a patient without the individual's consent, God will wait for you to trace your way back to His presence so that He can claim His fatherhood and authority over you as a child again. If you arrive and remain in His presence, how great then is your safety! You can rest your mind in the assurance that you are protected on every side and loaded with every benefit that your destiny requires.

Being back in His presence means being back at your full potential and at the peak of your *time of life*. The Amplified version of the verse has times *of refreshing (of recovering from the effects of heat, reviving with fresh air, restoring you like a cool wind on a hot day)* ... . Going into your sinful ways exposes you to heat, pain and sorrow, which can pose serious threat to your life. But the good news is that He will compensate you from whatever loss you might have suffered.

The recovery brings you back to the man (or woman)—*the you* that He created with great vitality, strength, righteousness and good heart. It brings you back to your best and maintains you there. It cancels away the scars and heals the wounds that wandering away has brought you. The recovery can only come when your time of refreshing comes. Your time of refreshing can only come when your *time of life* comes. The latter is a product of His *"go in peace"* which will not come before His *"Thy sins are forgiven"*. To achieve *Thy sins are forgiven*, you must initiate the *return* process and act out your part for Him to step into your case.

Chapter 8

The Purpose of Hard Times

We saw earlier that God does not and cannot forget anything or any person. *Remembered* (as seen in *Gen. 30 vs. 22, and 1 Sam 1 vs. 19*) can then be safely interpreted as *The Lord then decided, became ready, became moved to answer their prayers.* He that told Abraham *I will certainly return unto thee according to the time of life* must have known about those times of infertility as of *no life*. What is important here is that God does not and can never forget anyone. He is not just the all-knowing God, He knows all things before they happen and knows how all things will end.

At various intervals where I asked *why*, the Holy Spirit answered my questions. That is what chapter 8 will focus on—to know that there is at least a purpose for those seeming hard times.

The Relationship Comes First to Him

> *After these things the word of the LORD came unto Abram in a vision, saying, fear not, Abram; I am thy shield, and thy exceeding great reward. (Gen 15 vs. 1 KJV)*

The Time of Life

The opening phrase: *After these things* in the verse is loaded with many of the events that had taken place in the life of Abraham. As part of *these things*, he left his native land without hesitation; he dealt with Lot carefully; he got confirmation in the covenant (*13 vs. 14-18*); he fought and conquered; he dealt carefully with the king of Sodom and had been blessed by Melchizedek. Abraham's priority in all *these things* was building and sustaining a good and lasting relationship with God. Though the birth of Isaac was the next thing in Abraham's heart (*15 vs. 2-3*), the next level in God's diary were the achievements that the relationship should produce.

God, on many occasions, spoke and reassured Abraham concerning the birth of Isaac. But what I found so odd was:

> *And when Abram was ninety years old and nine, the LORD appeared to Abram, and said unto him, I am the Almighty God; walk before me, and be thou perfect (Gen. 17 vs. 1).*

As if it was still necessary for God to remind Abraham that He is God, He added the word *Almighty* as if to say *I can do with your case the humanly impossible.* He added a significant clause to seal the deal—*walk before me and be thou perfect.* I later observed the bridge between *Gen 15 vs. 1* and *17 vs. 1*. Sarah had suggested an alternative in *Gen 16*. So, walking before

The Purpose of Hard Times

God was not all that God required of Abraham but walking perfectly. All He was concerned with was ensuring the relationship was secure and vibrant. If delaying answers to your prayers would be the wisdom to keep you true to the relationship, then He would not do less than that. He does not just want you to relate with Him; He wants a relationship with you for which there will not be an alternative.

> *And the LORD appeared unto him in the plains of Mamre; and he sat in the tent door in the heat of the day ... And the LORD, said, shall I hide from Abraham that thing which I do...? (Gen 18 vs. 1, 17 KJV).*

God had transformed His relationship with Abraham into a friendship so much so that He, accompanied by His angels, visited Abraham in physical form, ate in his house, declared what was about to happen and then confided in him. The question in *vs. 17* was not answered, but then it appeared as if God meant *definitely I cannot hide anything from Abraham.* God's priority, I want to believe, was taking the friendship to the highest level attainable, regardless whether Isaac was forthcoming as expected or not. It is then crucial to address here that at the peak of our relationship with God, the answers to our prayers and the arrival of our *times of life* will become spontaneous and necessary. He has you in mind; please do not forget that.

Time of Life and God's Programme

Aside establishing and sustaining a functional relationship, it must also be said that the time of life does not come on request, but by necessity. Events have been programmed in God's realm long before they become manifest to us. God had foreseen what the Israelites would pass through in Egypt and that there would be a need for Joseph. He must have programmed Rachel to be the mother of such a son of destiny. I want to believe that the delay in bearing Joseph was worth it, if one considers his achievements and glory as the first prime minister of Egypt.

§ § §

> *For, lo, thou shalt conceive, and bear a son; and no razor shall come on his head: for the child shall be a Nazarite unto God from the womb; and he shall begin to deliver Israel out of the land of the Philistines (Judges 13 vs. 5 KJV)*

Regardless of how painful and disappointing Samson's parents found those years of barrenness, God was not set to give them merely a *time of life*, but a time of glory as well. *Time of life* becomes a time of glory if it comes at the time it is needed. Of several families that did not go barren in Israel, God could have raised a deliverer. But in line with His timing on the deliverance of His people, the destined parents of the to-be-deliverer had to wait in barrenness. The destiny of the *time of life* will make it wait for the season when there will be a need for it. The programmer in this context is God who will not stop at anything to fulfill His plans. Anchoring us into the story of Samson is *Judges 13 vs. 1* which tells of the existing situation prior to Samson's birth and *vs.* 5 offers the explanation of the relationship between the destiny of the child and the existing events.

> *Therefore also, I have lent him to the LORD; as long as he liveth he shall be lent to the LORD. And he worshipped the LORD there ... And Elkanah went to Ramah to his house. And the child did minister unto the LORD before Eli the priest . . . But Samuel ministered before the LORD, being a child, girded with a linen ephod... (I Sam 1 vs. 28, 2 vs. 11, 18 KJV)*

Except for Jacob, who was the second of a set of twins, the generals that were produced from barren women were a set of firstborns that did great exploits. Those wombs were not "shut up" because God was wicked, but because it was in line with His timing and the needs of His people. There had been priests before the birth of Samuel, but God knew that the destiny of His people was going to take a new turn for which a prophet like Samuel, would be needed. So, a woman, a family rather, had to wait. I imagine that it was hard for Hannah to let go of Samuel, having gone through those years of barrenness. But what she needed was no longer a child or children under her tent. After all, Elkanah was worth more than ten sons to her. What was needed in her heart was vindicating herself in face of her adversary, so it became easy for Samuel to be offered back to God, even early in his childhood days. For Elkanah's part, it is worth noting that the boy Samuel would not have been released to the priesthood without his consent. Aside from the relationship between the programmed need and your *time of life*, the *time of life* that you cannot dedicate to God or that you cannot use to glorify God, may not come until you recognise this. If no one will grant you a request that they know you will eventually use to attack them or that will draw you away from them, then the omniscient God will not either.

Hannah had been praying in previous years at Shiloh, but the pouring out of her heart on this occasion and her vows to God were of great effect. Although we had agreed that Samuel was coming at the time of his need in Israel, the place of Hannah's vow in orchestrating the deal is equally crucial.

> *And thou shalt have joy and gladness; and many shall rejoice at his birth. For he shall be great in the sight of the Lord, and shall drink neither wine nor strong drink; and he shall be filled with the Holy Ghost, even from his mother's womb. And many of the children of Israel shall he turn to the Lord their God. And he shall go before him*

> *in the spirit and power of Elias, to turn the hearts of the fathers to the children, and the disobedient to the wisdom of the just, to make ready a people prepared for the Lord. (Lk 1 vs. 14-17 KJV)*

The purpose of John the Baptist's birth was to prepare a people for the coming of the Messiah. It is, therefore, important to understand that his birth would in no doubt be delayed until the time of the Lord's birth. Thus, we see here another couple having to wait until they were well into years before their desires were granted, simply because their *time of life* must align to the need for the *time of life*.

Imagine the joy of Zacharias and Elizabeth to see their son grow to be relevant in the land. When the time of life comes, one's relevance becomes difficult to hide; one's role in fulfilling the prophecy becomes obvious. But if you can picture the gladness that must have been in the hearts of John's parents, then you must keep in mind that they were *well-stricken in years* before Elizabeth gave birth to John. They waited a long time.

The purpose of your seeming hard time is just to make sure your *time of life* happens when it is needed and will add glory to your essence. John the Baptist did not arrive in this world until it was the set time for his purpose (Jesus) to arrive. I understand how frustrating waiting can be, but it is a necessity. Samson's manifestation had to wait, just as John had to wait until the arrival of Jesus. Let it be known to you that "need" is the crucial issue that determines the season and *time of life*.

To Prevent You from Straying Away

> *And it came to pass, when Pharaoh had let the people go, that God led them not through the way of the land of the Philistines although that was near, for God said, Lest peradventure the people repent when they see war, and they return to Egypt... Thou shalt not bow down thyself to them, nor serve them: for I the LORD thy God, I am a jealous God.... (Ex 13 vs. 17; 20 vs. 5(a) KJV)*

Indeed, God will go to any length to keep His people to Himself. Being a jealous deity, He would not mind if you will have to go through the wilderness to reach the Red Sea. Whether your journey is long or short is not a priority to Him. How quickly or easily you arrive at your destination is not paramount to Him. His priority is to keep you near Him exclusively; to make you recognise Him as your God above all. His love for the children of Israel was no doubt the best possible. His ability to conquer the Philistines was also doubtless and potent. But in this context, guarding His people against anything that can turn their hearts from His plan was God's priority.

The Purpose of Hard Times

Was it not strange that these Israelites had to go through the wilderness, only to be stranded at the Red Sea? They had to face the terrible shock of being trapped in between the Red Sea in the front, and the pharaoh with his chariots behind. They must have concluded that they were going to die, seeing no route of escape.

Apart from the possibility of the Israelites warring with the Philistines, the outcome of the wars might also be a discouragement for the children of Israel. He does not want you to 'repent' against His plan for you. He will not mind leading you on a more difficult route regardless of the wilderness and the Red Sea, just to ensure you remain steadfast to Him. Aside from the desire of God to ensure that His people do not lose heart on their journey to the promised land, there is another precious purpose in God's chosen route.

> *And the LORD said unto Moses, when thou goest to return into Egypt, see that thou do all these wonders before Pharaoh, which I have put in thine hand; but I will harden his heart, that he shall not let the people go. And thou shalt say unto Pharaoh, Thus saith the LORD, Israel is my son, even my firstborn. And I say unto thee, Let my son go, that he may serve me: and if thou refuse to let him go, behold I will slay thy son, even thy firstborn. (Ex 4 vs. 21-23 KJV)*

> *And behold, I will harden the hearts of the Egyptians, and they shall follow them: and I will get me honour upon Pharaoh, and upon his entire host, upon his chariots, and upon his horsemen. And the Egyptians shall know that I am the LORD, when I have gotten me honour upon Pharaoh, upon his chariots, and upon his horsemen. (Ex 14 vs. 17-18 KJV)*

The Lord used the Israelites as bait to trap for the pharaoh and his men in the Red Sea. Many times in the book of *Exodus* (between *chapters 4 and 14*), God used the word *harden* to describe what He was going to do to the pharaoh's heart. He did not consider the entire population of Egyptians as more precious than His own firstborn—Israel. What a title! God did not just refer to Israel as His son but as His *firstborn son*. That means for years, the pharaoh and his men used God's firstborn as slaves, and from the point of sending Moses, He gave out His mission in clear words: *to bring freedom to His people at all cost and command His deserved honour from the Egyptians.*

That they may serve me was the primary purpose why God must free His people and the secondary was to get His honour from the pharaoh. To achieve His primary purpose, the Israelites did not pass through the nearer land of the Philistines but through the wilderness. To realise the second purpose, the people

The Purpose of Hard Times

of God had to come to the Red Sea. The third purpose I later got to comprehend was:

> *And Israel saw that great work which the LORD did upon the Egyptians; and the people feared the LORD, and believed the LORD, and his servant Moses. (Ex 14 vs. 31)*

God will go to any extent in His attempt to have His people revere and believe in Him. He did not eventually have His honour from the Egyptians alone, He equally got reverence from His people. Yes, He did this to prevent His people from straying from His statutes and commandments; to get His deserved honour from the hands of a pagan generation; to have the Israelites believe in Him the more and fear Him the more.

If you are, by any interpretation, stuck within any wilderness, or you find yourself facing the Red Sea, do not conclude that your God has forsaken you. Rather, make use of your place as His child to do greater exploits. And if by any means, there are chariots pursuing you, *hold your peace; you will see them no more.* Your father only wants you to be unwavering in your faith to Him alone.

Testing Your Resolve

Besides the place of favour, if any historical Biblical character convinces us of how *staying put* (perseverance) can schedule one for greater heights, Ruth's (the great-grandmother of David) story does. The prizes in any race vary. The medal for the 100m dash has less worth than that of 200m, 400m, 800m, and of course, all these pale in significance when compared to the prize for a marathon.

Orpah ran a race that I will classify within the region of 400m. Her resolve was tested and she eventually counted her options on the literal ground and opted out of the race, but that was not Ruth. This Moabitess left her people and her gods completely when she got married to Mahlon. The normal vow even in today's marriage ends with *till death do us part*, but in Ruth's understanding, it read *regardless of if death do us part.*

> *And they lifted up their voice, and wept again; and Orpah kissed her mother in law; but Ruth clave unto her.... And Ruth said, intreat me not leave thee, or to return from following after thee: for whether thou goest, I will go; and where thou lodgest, I will lodge; thy people shall be my people, and thy God, my God... the LORD do so to me, and more also, if ought but death part thee and me. (Ruth 1 vs. 14-17 KJV)*

I was almost left to wonder if Ruth had actually married Mahlon or Naomi. Of course, she married Mahlon, only that she did not see his death as the end of her relationship with the mother-in-law; she knew Naomi was a Jewess and believed in one God. She did not enter into the marathon because of any future benefit. That hopelessness was her destiny was a fact not too hard to believe as Naomi even explained to her daughter-in-law in *Ruth 1 vs. 12-13*. Orpah obeyed the social laws of the Moabites and remained behind, and her name disappeared from the archive of achievers.

However, Ruth's resolve was put to test to check whether she deserved the prize that lie ahead of her or not. *Time of life* in some cases may not come at first intention, or even in if the person is well stricken in years. Sometimes, it comes after standing your ground against a couple of tides and challenges.

Your resolve, like a man enrolled in marathon, might have to be tested again and again. And your eventual victory will then not be based on God's covenant concerning you alone, but also on how firm your decision is to adhere to your course. In *Gen 32 vs. 24-30*, Jacob did not have his victory worked out by God's covenant only, but also by a resilient determination not to give up.

The experience of Ruth was similar on her way to greatness. Apart from persevering, I found out that Ruth was able to fend for their survival. Many times, we rely on God to do His own part, and we ignore our part of the process, which the *time of life* should follow. To have your *time of life*, prayers will be a basic requirement, but that must run alongside other aspects of your character upon which *time of life* shall be built. Mountain tops are filled almost every day of the week with different calibres of believers, raising their voices in different volumes as if God were deaf;

and repeating with a loud voice the same statement over a couple of times as if He, that created memory, might soon or easily forget their words.

Churches and worship centres are filled every Sunday and most Friday nights, with various believers in various outfits as if to mark the birthday ceremony of God. Being on mountain tops or hills, and attending vigils or Sunday services are definitely not in any way bad. A fervent prayer life and worshipping in the assembly of brethren are two essentials of our faith.

My passion in this context is that many of us lack the character that can provoke the *time of life* to manifest. The character of Ruth, her determination and firm resolve are what most believers lack. Following Naomi to Bethlehem was not the peak of her marathon of resolve, but proving to be of a sound character. Spend a moment to think on this: *do I have the character that can usher in my time of life?* It is necessary for you to be sincere with yourself at this juncture. Your *time of life* may not be in waiting for its need; it may be that you often quit the race too early. The generals that made it before you were not men who tired easily. And you cannot stand in the shadow of their testimonies with the way you get easily fatigued. You have got to brace up! **There is a champion in you**, persevere your course, challenges notwithstanding.

That He Might be Glorified

The Purpose of Hard Times

> *When Jesus heard that, he said, this sickness is not unto death, but for the glory of God, that the son of God might be glorified thereby. (John 11 vs. 4 KJV)*

As established earlier, the good relationship between Jesus and Lazarus and his sisters, should have been enough to prevent Lazarus' death. The emotions displayed by Christ at the grave-side of Lazarus and how He addressed him in *vs. 11* showed how important their friendship was.

We thoroughly reviewed the events in *vs. 2-3* and the irony of Jesus' love for Lazarus by staying two extra days after receiving the news of his sickness. The notable point here is that Jesus was following the events in Lazarus' house (*vs. 11*) and did not hesitate to announce the death of His friend to His disciples. The course of events that culminated in the raising of Lazarus shows how Jesus had been very close to them when the going was good. But the question of why Jesus would allow His friend, whom He loved, to die, has not stopped throbbing my heart. The verse below is the answer to that question.

> *And I am glad for your sakes that I was not there, to the intent ye may believe; nevertheless let us go unto him.... . And I know that thou hearest me always; but because of the people which standby I said it, that they may believe that thou has sent me.... (John 11 vs. 15, 42 KJV)*

The Time of Life

Then gathered the chief priests and the Pharisees and the council, and said, what do we? For this man doeth many miracles. (John 11 vs. 47 KJV)

He might in your own context be aware and allow your predicaments in order for a council of pagans to recognise His potent power and ascribe more honour to Him. A mistake you must not make is to think you are too precious a jewel for Him to *experiment* with or use as a glory-generating channel. If He decided to use His dear Lazarus, then you must not consider your case as an exception. Glory is His food and currency and it will eventually become a privilege for you to be His channel. *Come forth, loose him, and let him go.*

Chapter 9

Farsightedness:
A Necessity for the Time of Life

Is not the whole land before thee? Separate thyself, I pray thee, from me: if thou wilt take the left hand, then I will go to the right: or if thou depart to the right hand, then I will go to the left. And Lot lifted up his eyes, and behold all the plain of Jordan, that it was well watered everywhere... then Lot chose him all the plain of Jordan; and Lot journeyed east and they separated themselves the one from the other. Abram dwelled in the land of Canaan, and Lot dwelled in the cities of the plain, and pitched his tent toward Sodom. (Gen. 13 vs. 9-23 KJV)

As a nephew to Abraham, Lot had been with Abraham for years and had become prosperous under his influence. Their herds and herdsmen had greatly increased and, as we can understand, there came up issues between the herdsmen of Abraham and Lot, that if it had not been well handled, could have caused a breach in their relationship. Consequently, Abraham sought to ensure that both of them had enough space to grow and still maintain their relationship. I consider Abraham wise and selfless in the way he handled Lot. He gave him the chance to choose first and this pleased Lot.

What could Lot have done better? There were some important things he could have done to guarantee his future of greatness. He could have given the opportunity to choose back to Abraham with humility, letting his uncle know that he was too young to have such a great privilege. He could have pleaded with Abraham to do the allocation and thereby save his head. Had Abraham been told politely to assign the lots, things could have gone a different direction. I also expected him to have requested for time to think through his choice. The opportunity to choose was so juicy to him that he did not ask for time to think through it or give back the first choice to Abraham.

A columnist published his weird observation concerning the former president of Nigeria, Goodluck Jonathan, in a weekly editorial—in September, 2010. He concluded that the lucky president, Goodluck Jonathan, often failed in situations where he had to take a decision within minutes or in an emergency. The

Farsightedness: A Necessity for the Time of Life

writer gave many instances in which the response of the president of the largest black nation did not match the global expectations of a man in such high position. But the fair side of the story is that he affirmed that Jonathan did something better than most other leaders in the nation's history—he bought time, as much as he had the privilege to do, and that he often came up with good decisions afterwards.

Hopefully, some columnists will do similar analysis of Jonathan's successor so we can see his score card. Buying time in order to come up with a sound decision was how the wise and famous King Solomon made it. Time was the secret behind the success of President Barack Obama. Solomon bought enough time. Every time he had to decide, he consulted elders, counsellors, and wise men that stood before his father David. Consequently, it did not take long for his wisdom to become known. Despite his oratory prowess, Obama bought time to seek counsel and ruminate on issues. Defeating Senator Hillary Rodham Clinton and John McCain was a product of this.

Lot did not buy time—not at least to go and pray. There was no time that the Bible recorded Lot conversing with God or His angels, save the time Sodom was to be destroyed.

He depended so much on his sight: *And Lot lifted up his eyes.* I would have expected the man that had lived with Abraham this long to lift up his heart or his voice, but he lifted up his eyes and worse, not to the Lord. You must trust God and his instructions to guide your steps. If you consult a world-famous ophthalmologist, to get the most potent of pair of eye glasses or have the best vision (eye function), your eyes will still not be as reliable as God's words. Abraham dwelled in the land but Lot relocated to the cities of the plain. What a relocation! That is the problem with most of us now. Relocating from one country or town to the other in search for better economy and social structures is now a daily event across the globe. And while that is not bad in itself, the major concern is that even the so-called believers also do this without regard for what God is saying.

The *time of life* does not depend on how small or great your place of origin. It does not even depend on how good the socioeconomic standard of your city or country. It is not where you are, but who is with you. If you must obtain the time of life, you must then learn and adapt with the rules of location. It is left to be seen whether you have been divinely positioned in that seemingly lowly place or not. The so-called cities of the plain may offer a glamorous lifestyle, but all that glitters is not gold. If you must relocate, then lift up your heart, your voice, and your eyes unto the Lord for His guidance and presence.

Escape for Thy Dear Life

> *And they took Lot, Abram's brother's son, who dwelt in Sodom, and his goods and departed. (Gen 14 vs. 12)*

Farsightedness: A Necessity for the Time of Life

> *For we will destroy this place, because the cry of them is waxen great before the face of the LORD; and the LORD hath sent us to destroy it.... And it came to pass, when they had brought them forth abroad, that he said, Escape for thy life; look not behind thee, neither stay thou in all the plain; escape to the mountain, lest thou be consumed. (Gen. 19 vs. 13, 17 KJV)*

The cities of the plain that had attracted Lot's attention had become where Lot must flee from. Before the angel's arrival to destroy Sodom, Abraham had become a man of war. Lot would have lost his identity, goods and family had his uncle, Abraham, not come to his aid.

The cities of the plain, first of all, became cities of captivity for Lot. I do not think Lot experienced any form of growth while in Sodom. Abraham negotiated with God to save Sodom, given there were up to 10 upright persons in the city, perhaps, because of Lot. Although God did not get up to ten persons, Lot had the rare privilege to have been led out of the cities by the angels.

What amazed me was the request of Lot to relocate to the city of Zoar, not the mountain. A mountain is a place of prominence. Lot, however, preferred valleys and plains as long as they are cities. I felt so much pity for him. He lost his courage while living in the city, so much so, that he had to dwell in the cave of Zoar. Worse for him was how he ended being the father of children from his own daughters—the result of how city life had altered the moral standards of Lot and his daughters. If you are in Sodom, you cannot experience a *time of life*; you must *escape for thy life*.

Exceeding Multiplication of the "Wild Man"

> *Now Sarai, Abram's wife, bare him no children: and she had a handmaid, an Egyptian, whose name was Hagar. And Sarai said into Abram, behold now, the LORD hath restrained me from bearing; I pray thee, go in unto my maid; it may be that I may obtain children by her. And Abram hearkened to the voice of Sarai.*
> (Gen. 16 vs. 1-2 KJV)

Not all kindness is profitable to your time of life. All attempts to create a shortcut in the course of your *time* will only bring long-cuts and adverse effects. It is not a controversial point that Sarah meant well for Abraham. I supposed Sarah was about 75 years old and Abraham around 85 when she came up with this idea. Sarah must have given up on her own fertility that she wanted an alternative to ensure they had a child. She advised Abraham accordingly, but he did not ask from Lord. He failed to buy time for detailed consideration. *He hearkened to the voice of Sarai* and took Hagar as wife. Hagar was probably no longer seen as a maid.

She was no longer a handmaid but a *bedmaid*—a baby-making machine. As if to prove that Abraham and Sarah had taken the right decision, Hagar had no challenge conceiving for Abraham.

I did not find it hard to comprehend the change in the character of Hagar. I rather found it amazing that Sarah did not prepare for the altercation that was to follow. Hagar's estimation of Sarah changed and her mistress became despised in her eyes. This brought about a chain of events that justified Sarah's outburst on Abraham. *My wrong be upon thee... and the LORD Judge between me and thee* was Sarah's emotional cry (*vs. 4-6*).

To safeguard his marriage and his image, Abraham had no option than to declare Sarah as judge who is to do with her maid whatsoever she pleases. Like every other woman in Sarah's capacity would do, she dealt harshly with Hagar so that Hagar had to *escape for her life*. What Abraham would have done had he been the judge over this case is something one can only imagine.

The One Who programmed your time of life will cater for all aspects of it. Waiting might sometimes appear frustrating, but as much as I know, great exploits are products of great patience in the lives of great waiters. The word *alternative* does not exist in God's lexicon. You would have heard preachers or motivational speakers talking about *spare parts*, probably when counselling converts. Whether the teaching is right or not is not our concern here. But even if there were spare parts in God's treasury, there are no alternatives to *the time of life*. Alternatives only exist with humans, in which case you may want to try another option, when one becomes unsuitable, comes too late or fails to come at all. The things that force us to seek alternatives are not applicable to God. He has programmed all things to their corresponding times; no lateness or delay with Him. That which you term as late is timely in His agenda. However positive, you may define the word alternative, in God's context, it is 'altering-native'. The program-mer of nature is the only capable One to order nature, and any attempt by you will only run into crisis. You cannot alter nature and not give birth to a wild man.

> *And the angel of the LORD said unto her, behold, thou art with child, and shalt bear a son, and shall call his name Ishmael: because the LORD hath heard thy affliction. And he will be a wild man; his hand will be against every man; and every man's hand against him; and he shall dwell in the presence of all his brethren. (Gen 16 vs. 11-12)*

> *And Sarah saw the son of Hagar the Egyptian, which she had born unto Abraham, mocking. Wherefore she said unto Abraham, cast out this bondwoman and her son: for the son of this bondwoman shall not be heir with my son, even with Isaac. And this thing was very*

Farsightedness: A Necessity for the Time of Life

grievous in Abraham's sight because of his son. (Gen. 21 vs. 9-11 KJV)

Originally, the word *wild* was only used for animals. But here, it is used to describe the *alternative* son of Abraham, Ishmael. Apart from being described as *wild*, he was also declared to be against nature in that every man's hand shall at all times be against him and vice versa. Worse still, he shall dwell in the presence of his brethren, waging wars. What more or less can we expect of Ishmael?

However, God extended His kindness and greatness to this "wild son" because he was an offspring of Abraham, God's covenanted friend *(Gen. 16 vs. 19, 13, and 21 vs. 12-18)*. If Ishmael will then become great in life, he will definitely also become great in his wildness. If a nation had been promised to come from him, it must, of course, be a wild nation. This explains what the world is witnessing today in the civil strife of the nations that came out of Ishmael's loins.

Our earlier suggestion that we could only imagine what Abraham's handling of the fracas between Sarah and Hagar is answered in *Gen. 21 vs. 11-12*. Sarah must have been demanding too much and too often in the sight of Abraham. Before Isaac was born, the pregnancy of Hagar created quite a fracas in the household.

Ishmael, the son of Hagar, was fourteen (14) when Isaac, the son of the covenant was born *(Gen. 16 vs. 16; 21 vs. 5)* This kindled another reaction from Sarah.

She wanted wanted Hagar and Ishmael out of the household in order to create enough space for Isaac. *O that Ishamel might live before thee!* was the response of Abraham when God reminded him of the coming of Isaac. Now that Isaac had arrived, the mind set of Abraham, as *Gen. 21 vs. 11-12* would have us imagine, would be *O that Ishmael and Isaac, his younger brother, might live before thee O God.* A *co-heir* and elder brother was what Sarah does not want for the son of her 90th year. But was she not the one who orchestrated Ishmael? Yes, she was. But such was the regret her alternative brought her.

No matter how fulfilling you might feel with the alternative, you will have regrets combining it with the original at the *time of life.* And to avoid creating problems that might mar or even terminate your joy at your *time of life,* it becomes paramount to avoid alternatives. Rather, wait for your time of life. Do not seek its *altered-nature.*

Time of Life Brings Back Your Audience

Footballers and their coaches, actors and their producers, the mass media and their personnel, politicians and comrades are a few of the classes of people who can attract a crowd in today's world. To sportsmen, it is a great source of inspiration. This is so for others too. Saul, the son of Kish, had become king following the request of the people of God for a king. We will consider how Saul lost God because he wanted to retain his audience.

Farsightedness: A Necessity for the Time of Life

> *And he tarried seven days, according to the set time that Samuel had appointed; but Samuel came not to Gilgal; and the people were scattered from him. And Saul said; bring hither a burnt offering to me, and peace offerings. And he offered the burnt offering. And it came to pass, that as soon as he had made an end of offering the burnt offering, behold, Samuel came; and Saul went out to meet him, that he might salute him. (1 Sam 13 vs. 8-10 KJV)*

Samuel had committed himself to return to Gilgal for the work of the office of the priest in seven days but he arrived a bit late. The duration of the lateness was not stated but the thing here was the audacity that Saul had to perform the assignment of a priest, as if the offering had a time limitation. He acted as if he did not have enough knowledge of the rules and principles of the priestly office. *Disobedience* and *pressure* are two reasons scholars have provided to explain King Saul's erroneous act. However, another reason that is applicable to this context is *impatience*. Saul's impatience, combined with his need to keep up with human timing led him to violate the orderliness that worshipping God in that context entailed.

The Hearing

> *And Samuel said, what hast thou done? And Saul said, because I saw that the*

> *people were scattered from me, and that thou camest not within the days appointed, and that the Philistines gathered themselves together at Michmash; therefore said I, The Philistines will come down now upon me to Gilgal, and I have not made supplication unto the LORD; I forced myself therefore, and offered a burnt offering. (vs. 11-12 KJV)*

Samuel did not conclude the case of Saul before hearing him out even though none of his reasons were good enough to have made him commit such error. *Thou camest not* as if to mean that Samuel was not forthcoming and there was little or no hope of his imminent arrival. *I saw that the people were scattered from me* as if to mean that going against God's will to retain his crowd was the ideal. What must be understood here is that you cannot do the right assignment at a wrong time, with the wrong personnel, in the wrong place, and for the wrong reason. All these made Saul's seemingly right intention wrong in its entirety. If the king would use the word "forced" to describe the pressure, then, the question will be: "Who forced whom?" King Saul forced himself. No, not the pressure of the looming Philistines, but his impatience.

Avoid Being Foolish and Your Time of Life Will Continue

Farsightedness: A Necessity for the Time of Life

> *And Samuel said to Saul, thou hast done foolishly: thou hast not kept the commandment of the LORD thy God, which he commanded thee; for now would the LORD have established thy kingdom upon Israel forever. But now thy kingdom shall not continue: the LORD has sought him a man after his own heart, and the LORD hath commanded him to be captain over his people, because thou has not kept that which the LORD commanded thee ... . (vs. 13-14 KJV)*

Looking deeply into how the Israelites had unanimously requested to have a king *(I Sam 8 vs. 11-22)*, Samuel told them the good and the bad side of having a king. Damning the consequences, the children of Israel persisted on their request. The man God sought for Himself in the person of Saul was not this foolish man. Something must have gone wrong with his original nature. God is a wise deity who will select the best for Himself every time there is the need for a person. I perceive that Saul would have been the fairest at that time in Israel.

However, here is the man being declared a fool. I took a detailed look at the verses above and I concluded that Samuel did not pronounce his judgment based on any personal dislike for Saul or for performing a priest's duty. The judgment was based on the violation of God's commandments. Samuel stressed the premise of his declaration which was the violation of God's commandments. According to Samuel, it was outright foolishness for a renowned and respected king to have gone against the words and charges of God. He then went ahead to sound out the bad side of the story for Saul: *For now would the LORD have established thy kingdom upon Israel forever.*

I want to assume that Samuel would have confirmed the kingship of Saul that same day had he not fallen into this foolishness. We do not know why Samuel arrived late, but had Saul waited for him, he would have had a testimony to show for the waiting. In your course of life, you must learn to be reliant on God's time frame, outside which you can only meet failure.

Foolishness has a price; the worth of which a lifetime of wisdom might not be able to undo. The price in Saul's situation was the termination of his regime. He became impatient, and that meant the end of his reign as King of Israel. Worse for him was the fact that God sought another man to replace Saul while he was still on the throne. In attaining your greatness in life and in bringing your *time of life* into reality, you must learn to wait, and you must adhere strictly to God's instructions. Impatience with God's time frame is the fastest route to your pitfall. You can avoid being foolish if you so wish and obeying God is the premise upon which you are to build your *time of life*. It is wisdom to obey God, and all other things you hope to have in life will become spontaneous afterwards.

Chapter 10

Nevertheless

The *time of life* that most people anticipate will be kept waiting until they confess *nevertheless* in surrender. 'Nevertheless', means *in spite of something*. The word appears 97 times in the Bible but the one from Peter caught my attention.

> *And Simon answering said unto him, master, we toiled all the night, and have taken nothing: nevertheless at thy word I will let down the net and when they had this done, they inclosed a great multitude of fishes: and their net brake. (Lk 5 vs. 5-6 KJV)*

Peter and his fellow fishermen had worked all night, coasted the sea and waited for a harvest of fishes, but that night was not just theirs. As skilful as Peter was,

The Time of Life

he could not boast of a fish for that sleepless night. The master requested that Peter let down his nets, not for another unprofitable attempt, but *for a draught* of harvest. Peter made Jesus understand their effort and how fruitless the night had been, as if the All-knowing did not know their situation. But he went a mile ahead by issuing a *nevertheless*. Peter, with this, did not entirely agree something was possible; that was why he offered an explanation before his *nevertheless*. Peter's response was like *I know we cannot achieve anything with this trial but I won't argue with you on this*. That decision not to argue with Jesus was the only thing needed for their night to be most fruitful. Submitting to His words, as odd or unrealistic as they were, they were paid off with a great harvest.

To make it in life and to attain your desired *time of life*, you must face a crucial hurdle in the process of submitting your will at His feet. I am convinced that many people would have done better and gone farther had they uttered their *nevertheless* earlier in life in response to God's commands. His words and commands may not look to be the most attractive. It may, in fact, look impossible to be real; it may not be as refined as you would prefer. But the hidden truth is that His words and commands are not just the best for your life, they are also the most suitable for your needs. In the face of challenges, when soothing words fail to materialise immediately—as in the case of

Abraham, *"Nevertheless I will wait on you"* will seem the most appropriate from you.

Peter, it appeared, would not have lost anything had they not catch fishes at His command. They already accepted their fate as regards that night, but they would have lost *a great multitude of fishes* had they disobeyed.

That night's miracle came the moment Peter issued that clause as he travelled back and forth between his factual knowledge and his surrender to Christ's will. To make your destiny count and to bring in that *time of life*, it is necessary for you to confess your *nevertheless*, letting go of your hold in order to submit to His position. You really need to know that others might even mock you, frustrate you and persecute you for becoming so foolish in agreeing to do the seemingly impossible and unrealistic. You must be convinced that holding unto His word will vindicate you, with time.

At Thy Word, I Will . . .

So many prayers may never be answered until we change our stand and action. The change in our stand is to first move closer to Him and then train our ears to know and hear His voice. It is possible that Peter's role could have been filled by another fisherman if Jesus had no destiny to keep with the Rock. And by a few erroneous decisions, Peter could have prevented their relationship from ever taking place.

> *And saw two ships standing by the lake but the fishermen were gone out of them and were washing their nets. And he entered into one of the ships, which was Simon's, and prayed him that he would thrust out a little from the land. And he sat down, and taught the people out of the ship. (Lk 5 vs. 2-3)*

Peter had a choice to make—whether to allow or disallow Him, Who made all things, from using His ship for the teaching session. Had Peter denied Him, of course, another fisherman would have granted Jesus His request. If you do His will, you will, at last, have nothing to lose. But not doing His will bring you to lose everything. Those aspects of your calling, career and destiny will experience abundance if you would only allow Him to *use your ship* for His purpose. You will have to let go to Him of your stern grip in some areas you are still holding on to in order to usher in your *time of life*.

Another *nevertheless* expressed in word and in action was the prayer of Jesus in *Lk 22 vs. 42: Father, if thou be willing, remove this cup from me: nevertheless not my will, but thine, be done.*

Jesus would have loved to have the *cup* removed from Him at that moment, but He submitted to the will of the Father. If the Saviour could submit to the will of His Father and pray His will be done, it is then compulsory for us, too, to submit to the will of God.

Many times we offer prayer points that are not in His plans for our lives. We sweat so much praying amiss and asking for those things we do not need. Christ had His own will, but He knew and submitted to His Father's.

To ask correctly, it is important to first know His plans for your life so as to ensure that all you ask in prayer goes in line with His will for you. Always ensure that you are asking for the right things by praying the Holy Spirit to help you out on occasions of need.

To Get Your Attention

However faulty your attention to Him might be, God wants to deal with you in such a way as to have your attention to Himself alone. He wants you to know that He is God and that He reigns over all. The earlier you get to know and comply with this, the better for you. Jonah's story is the summary of what God can do to arrest a man's attention. Jonah would have saved himself a lot of stress had he given out his *nevertheless*. A *nevertheless* would have saved Zachariah from being rendered dumb had he resisted the urge to argue with the angel. Confessing your *nevertheless* will go a long way to safeguard your comfort and usher in your greatness.

Sometimes, the *nevertheless* is what lies between you and your destiny. Peter, from that point, was bought over completely by Christ. He was also caught by the effect of that *nevertheless*: *Fear not: from henceforth thou shalt catch men.* (Lk 5 vs. 10(b) KJV).

Had Peter denied Christ his ship, and argued with Him without a *nevertheless*, only God can tell what would have become of His entire ministry and destiny.

He Wants What You Hold Dear

What He wants is what you reserve most to yourself. His plan is to assume the position of that which you crave for the most. He had to get Abraham's LOVE and attention before giving him Isaac. That was why Abraham did not rate Isaac more precious than God. He did not attempt to reserve his son and deny his God. Until you get to understand this, there is no length of time that is too long in God's diary to make you wait to learn the lesson.

www.ingramcontent.com/pod-product-compliance
Lightning Source LLC
Chambersburg PA
CBHW021709230426
43668CB00008B/778